CAREERS IN
CATERING, HOTEL
ADMINISTRATION
& MANAGEMENT

CAREERS IN
CATERING, HOTEL
ADMINISTRATION
& MANAGEMENT

Russell Joseph

sixth edition

**KOGAN
PAGE**

First published in 1983
Second edition 1985
Third edition 1989
Fourth edition 1993
Fifth edition 1997
Sixth edition 2000

Kogan Page Limited
120 Pentonville Road
London N1 9JN

© Kogan Page Limited, 1983, 1985, 1989, 1993, 1997, 2000

British Library Cataloguing in Publication Data

A CIP record for this book is available from the British Library.

ISBN 0 7494 3149 0

Typeset by Jean Cussons Typesetting, Diss, Norfolk
Printed and bound in Great Britain by Clays Ltd, St Ives plc

Contents

Contents

Foundation; Hotel and Catering International Management Association; Housekeepers' Association; Institute of Food Science and Technology; Institute of Home Economics; The Royal Institute of Public Health and Hygiene; Royal Society of Health; Training and Enterprise Councils and Local Enterprise Companies (various locations); Wine and Spirit Education Trust Ltd; Other useful addresses

Index 113

Introduction

Is this the Job for You?

❏ Would you like a job where you can learn skills that give you the opportunity to travel the world?

❏ Do you like working with people?

❏ Do you like variety?

❏ Can you endure hard work?

❏ Would you like to work in an expanding industry?

❏ Do you want to work in an industry where jobs are created daily?

❏ Do you want a job with real prospects for promotion?

❏ Would you like to work for a large hotel company such as Whitbread, Forte or Hilton, a restaurant chain such as Beefeater, Conran or Pelican, or a public house group such as Bass, Youngs or Allied Domecq?

❏ Do you want to learn how to run your own business?

❏ Would you like to meet celebrities such as David Beckham, Posh Spice or the Royal Family?

If you said 'yes' to the majority of questions, then a job in catering, hotel administration or management might be right for you.

◆ Do you want amazing employment opportunities?
◆ Do you want to learn skills that guarantee work?
◆ Do you like shift work?
◆ Do you like hard work?
◆ Do you like helping people enjoy themselves?
◆ Do you like being part of a team?

If you answered 'no' to any of the questions above, then perhaps this industry isn't right for you.

What is this industry all about?

When you order a meal in a restaurant, hotel or takeaway have you ever considered the number of people involved? Who takes your order, prepares and serves your food, takes your money, cleans the restaurant, washes up, controls the finances, orders the food from suppliers or employs staff?

When you arrive at an hotel have you ever thought about the reservation system, auditing and accounting, housekeeping and maintenance, conference facilities, functions and banqueting or even personnel?

The hotel, catering and hospitality industry can be described as including anything that involves the provision of accommodation, food or drink. It is one of the largest employers in the country with over two million employees in more than a quarter of a million outlets. It is a fast growing industry and, as such, employment prospects are increasing. Employers range from five-star hotels to guest houses, industrial caterers to fast food, airports to conferences. Job opportunities include chefs, managers, receptionists, personnel, waiting staff and bartenders, all available to men and women. Opportunities exist for all grades of staff, some who are qualified, a few who are not, and some who are studying and working at the same time.

There are many job opportunities in hotel administration,

catering and management for those with experience and qualifications. Those not qualified will still find employment although qualified staff are more likely to be paid higher wages and salaries and find the best jobs. Qualified staff may also have the opportunity to travel the world using their skills, such as a chef on a cruise ship or a barperson in a luxury holiday resort.

In addition to qualifications, many of the jobs in catering, hotel administration and management rely on a good personality, the ability to work hard for long hours and the need to work unsocial hours, not necessarily just nine to five. The jobs will mostly involve weekend work, giving time off during the week. Some of the conditions are poor, but in how many businesses will you be given the opportunity to travel with the skills you have learnt, be rewarded for effort and be employed in a growing industry?

2 Hotels, restaurants, motels and holiday camps

Which job is for me?

There are many opportunities for employment in hotel and catering and they exist both back- and front-of-house. Back-of-house jobs are usually not involved directly with the customers, for example chefs, kitchen assistants, kitchen porters, auditors and controllers. Front-of-house staff, many of whom are uniformed, are the first to have contact with guests and so must give a good impression. Such jobs include receptionists, waiting staff, reservation clerks, porters and department managers.

Hotel manager

A general manager (or GM) has to have some knowledge of each and every department within the hotel and usually will be assisted by a management team consisting of department heads. The GMs will probably have one or two specialist areas of knowledge reflecting their past experience. This may be as executive housekeeper or food and beverage manager, for example. They are responsible for the smooth running and financial success of the business. Managers must have the ability to plan, control and work within budgets and reach targets by using all the hotel's resources and delegating where necessary.

Case Study

Gillian Arnold *is a duty manager at the St. George's hotel in Coventry.*

'I didn't do very well at school but luckily I was allowed on to a BTEC National Diploma in Hotel and Catering. College was ok, but it wasn't until I went on work experience that I finally realized what hotel life was all about. Until then I had just imagined it, although I had been on holiday with my family staying in hotels. I suppose it was this that made me want a hotel career.

'The work experience was really good. The college mainly used three-star hotels. Their argument was that students would get a much better experience there, rather than at a luxury hotel who wouldn't let students loose on guests for fear of frightening them away. The hotel offered me a job at the end of the work experience, saying that they would train me and that I didn't need to go back to college to finish my course. I talked it over with my parents and decided that I needed to get a qualification. I went back to college and finally passed the course. The hotel was quite good about it and offered me a job at weekends and told me to apply when I qualified.

'After my final exams, I went on holiday with my parents to Spain. It was really good and I was introduced to the hotel manager after talking about my career to one of the holiday reps. He took a shine to me and offered me a job. I accepted and went to work on the Costa del Sol. I did loads of jobs including kitchen, restaurant, bar work and housekeeping. My Spanish improved too.

'After a year, I left Spain and worked in London as an assistant manager in a small hotel. It was part of a group of hotels and I started off in the smallest hotel as a junior. After just a few months, a job came up as assistant manager in one of the bigger hotels. I was offered the job.

'My current job was advertised in the *Caterer and Hotelkeeper*. It pays well and I have a good team of staff. We all get on well together and I think that is why we have been so successful, winning a local business prize. We have bad days too, like when the fire alarm kept going off and no one knew why. And again when the electricity went off just before a wedding party was due to arrive. But we have good times too.

'I plan on staying here for another year or two and then I might work abroad again. So far I have always specialized in "front-of-house" because of my liking for dealing with guests' problems, but I think I need to get more restaurant and kitchen experience. Eventually I want to open my own small hotel. Possibly somewhere where I can use my languages again.'

Food and beverage manager

This managerial position entails responsibility for the entire food and beverage operation within the hotel. The food and beverage manager will be in charge of areas of food production and service and beverage service, both alcoholic and non-alcoholic. The manager is responsible for all the staff, the work standards and the budget. Most managers have been promoted from restaurant manager and have a degree, Higher National Diploma, GNVQ Advanced qualification or NVQ in addition to experience.

Restaurant manager

The restaurant manager has responsibility for the entire restaurant and supervises all the staff in the area. This will include waiters, waitresses and cashiers. They are not normally responsible for the kitchen but work closely with the head or executive chef on matters such as menu content, pricing and budgets. They need to have good social skills to deal with the customers and be able to use sales and marketing skills to promote the restaurant and menu. It is likely that they will have extensive knowledge of alcoholic beverages. Many managers will have risen from the food service team. They may have a GNVQ Advanced or an NVQ level 3. Some may have completed the Wine and Spirit Education Trust examinations also. A second language is advantageous.

Case Study

Gordon Barton is the restaurant manager and host of the Stow, a popular restaurant in Essex.

'I originally went to college because I wanted to be a chef. At home, I was always cooking and a careers teacher suggested I go to college to do general catering. My nearest college was at Southend and I went there for two years. The course was really good; we did food preparation and theory, restaurant service, food hygiene and nutrition. We had two sessions in the training kitchen, one in the bakery department and one in the main kitchen. The pastry teacher was excellent. A friend of mine went on to open her own business in the area, Carol's Cakes. The college had a training restaurant where members of the public could book and come in for a meal. My first time was desperate. I was so nervous but was given a 50p tip, which really made my day.

'When I left, I went to work in Southend as a chef at the casino. It was my first true experience of a real kitchen. The head chef was really helpful and after a year, I got promoted. Three jobs later, I became the head chef at a restaurant, which was part of a big chain. Going from a single restaurant to a big company was a real shock.

'An estate agent friend bought a disused bank and wanted to turn it into a restaurant. I worked with him all through the planning stages and eventually we opened a successful business. I started in the kitchen and trained all the chefs into my way of working. We had a reputation for being quite adventurous and we used ingredients that were fairly new to the UK. I think we were the first by a long way to use rocket, judging by the customers' reactions. After two years, my partner wanted to move on and so I decided that I should move out of the kitchen and become the host or restaurant manager. This way I get to see all the customers, whereas it was different in the kitchen. However, I have to learn to control myself sometimes when some of the customers complain about really silly things. At least in the kitchen they couldn't see my reaction!

'The biggest problem I have is staff. Hard-working qualified people are hard to come by. But I like to think that when I find someone who is keen and willing, I give them as much support as they need, and if they need more training, they go to the college for a part-time course. The best member of staff is a chef who used to work in the City with a bank. He loved cooking, and when his bank made some redundancies, he took the plunge and changed careers at 31. I admire his enthusiasm and I am sure he will go far.

'I'm not sure what the future holds. The restaurant business is hard work, but I really enjoy it and I don't know what else I would want to do.'

Waiters

Waiters serve food and drink to customers. Depending on the restaurant, they may be highly skilled and be able to serve from silver platters. This is known as 'silver service'. Alternatively, they may just serve customers with food already on a plate from the kitchen. A good waiter will be able to remember who ordered each dish from a large party of guests or, in the case of regular guests, favourite dishes or drinks. Some restaurant waiters are employed part-time, supplementing their income with banqueting or function catering. A qualified waiter will possess NVQs in food service. Those hoping to progress to management will need either a GNVQ Advanced or a profile of NVQs and experience.

Chefs

Executive chefs are in charge of the kitchen and in large establishments may not cook any more, although most prefer to. It is a management position gained after working for many years. They will plan menus and discuss them with the hotel or restaurant manager, be responsible for food storage and control, order supplies and plan staffing levels. They will also be responsible for all the employees in the kitchen including other chefs, kitchen assistants and porters. They will need to work within a budget and ensure hygiene standards are maintained. Most executive chefs will have worked in a specialist area within the kitchen, prior to their promotion. They will be qualified with NVQs or equivalent, together with hygiene qualifications.

In a large traditional kitchen, the terminology is in French and the assistant chefs have titles and specialist areas. Duties may vary according to the establishment, but generally they are:

- *Sous Chef* – deputy head chef;
- *Chef Gardemanger* – in charge of the larder;
- *Chef Potager* – soups and stocks;
- *Chef Entremettier* – vegetable chef;
- *Chef Rôtisseur* – chef in charge of roasting;
- *Chef Poissonier* – fish chef;
- *Chef Saucier* – sauces and main meals;
- *Chef Pâtissier* – pastries, sweets, cakes and ice creams.

Each section leader, as above, is known as a *Chef de Partie*. They have a team of assistants or juniors known as commis chefs, who mostly have NVQs.

Case Study

Karen Wood *is a chef at the Beverly Hills Hilton in Los Angeles.*

'I completed an NVQ level 3 in Food Preparation in Bournemouth. The chef lecturer was excellent, even though I wasn't very good at some of the things we did. If I could pinpoint my specialization, it would be fish dishes and sauces, probably because of my training. Soon after college, I got a full-time job in a local hotel and stayed there for six months as a commis chef. A typical day would be starting work at 8 am and having a break in the afternoon, before starting work again. I think I learned a great deal about timings, making sure the food was at the right temperature, and looking its best. College had been much more relaxed than work. Sometimes a restaurant kitchen can be frantic.

'I wanted to travel and so went to London and worked in one of the restaurants owned by Mr Conran, who owns many restaurants. While working there, I met my husband, an American, who was working in England for two years. We married and I went back to the USA with him and found my current job.

'I get on really well with the head chef, and when he wanted to update the menu and develop a new style, he approached me for some ideas. We came up with the idea of East meets West, thus pleasing a cross-section of the clientele. We developed dishes incorporating Thai with Western ingredients and it has become very popular. Maybe it is the USA culture, but so many people here eat out rather than cook at home. The storekeeper here is good but I like to check all the ingredients myself when they are delivered. I even went to the fish market to meet the suppliers face to face so that they knew what I wanted and the quality too.

'The long-term plan is for us to open our own restaurant and this may be on the coast between here and San Francisco. The menu will incorporate organic ingredients, which are increasingly popular. I will be in the kitchen and my husband will be the host. Even though he enjoys cooking at home, he is much better as a salesperson than me and so we can use his strengths in the restaurant and mine in the kitchen. We are a good partnership.'

Kitchen porter or kitchen assistant

The kitchen porter is the person who washes the pots and pans in a kitchen and carries out heavy–duty cleaning of equipment. The job is often looked upon as having low status, yet it is one of the most important. Although most porters are unqualified, a knowledge of food hygiene is useful, as is the ability to work in a hot kitchen. Some kitchens employ kitchen assistants to carry out basic tasks, for example vegetable preparation. Most aspire to become cooks and chefs and use the opportunity to gain knowledge and experience.

Bar staff

Bar managers are in charge of one or more bars within the same establishment. They are responsible for the staff, equipment, supply of alcoholic and non-alcoholic beverages, and control procedures. This means that they have to control and supervise stocks of wine, beers and spirits. It is essential that they have a good working knowledge of the liquor licensing laws. They have to work within a budget and are financially accountable to a food and beverage manager or general manager, depending on the establishment. All will have had extensive experience as a bar person. The staff will usually include several bar persons, a cellarman and possibly a wine waiter. Bar persons serve drinks, take money, and ensure the bar area is clean. Cellarmen work in the cellars, looking after and keeping stock of beers and wines. The wine waiter is responsible to the head waiter. Currently, bar staff need to be over 18 to work behind a bar. There are NVQs levels 1 and 2 in beverage service and levels 3 and 4 in on-licensed premises supervisory management. Further information is available from the British Institute of Innkeeping.

Executive housekeeper

Executive housekeepers are in charge of all the accommodation and public areas of the hotel. This includes the servicing of the guests' bedrooms, the laundry room, linen room and lounge or lobby areas of the hotel. They will have a team of floor house-keepers who will be responsible for checking room maids' work and the standards of cleaning in the guests' bedrooms.

Many hotels now use a contract cleaning company for the public areas of the hotel, which are usually cleaned at night to avoid disturbing guests during the day and creating an untidy appearance. When hotels refurbish guests' rooms they often do it section by section. Executive housekeepers have to work with the contractors, ensuring that the rooms are fitted and furnished to the appropriate standard. They need to work within the constraints of the housekeeping budget. For example, they have to calculate whether it would be financially advantageous to use an outside company for laundry or use hotel staff. They also need to have an excellent knowledge of the science of cleaning, such as stain removal. Most housekeepers have at some stage in their careers worked as room maids before progressing to floor housekeepers and assistant head housekeepers. Most are qualified to BTEC National, GNVQ Advanced, or NVQ level 4 or higher in housekeeping. Many belong to the UK Housekeepers' Association.

Case Study

Noel Jaffray *is the executive housekeeper at a four-star hotel in Dublin.*

'At college, I did a BTEC National Diploma in Hotel and Catering, equivalent to a GNVQ Advanced. After passing the course, I went to university and successfully completing a degree in Hospitality Management. When I first went to college, I thought that there were only two sides to an hotel: the reception area and the food side. I didn't realize two important facts until much later on. Firstly, housekeeping is the biggest revenue provider for the business. Even if guests stay, it doesn't necessarily mean that they will eat in the hotel's restaurant. Secondly, housekeeping is a fast way to general management.

'I studied accommodation at college and rooms division at university and even did some work experience in the housekeeping department of an hotel, but my first job was in reservations and reception. It was part of a graduate training programme for an international hotel group. After the training, I saw in the hotel staff magazine that there was a floor housekeeping job available within the group. I wasn't too keen at first, thinking wrongly that it was a woman's job, but the hotel was the biggest and most prestigious in the group. I applied, was offered the job, and I really enjoyed it. Being in charge of room attendants, I had a real people management job. When the executive housekeeper went on maternity leave, the deputy was promoted and I was given her job. As luck would happen, she didn't return and I got the job full-time. By this time, I was already earning over £20,000 per year, much more than any of my old university friends.

'The work was hard, and some of the maids knew very little English. I used to spend my time off planning new ways to help them understand. Some of the work was bad; until you work in housekeeping, you don't realize how dirty some people are.

'Three years later, I applied for this job. The Emerald Isle is booming at the moment and I think that is why I chose to apply. There are so many opportunities in hotels here and I believe it has helped me move up the management chain faster. Saying this makes me seem ruthless, but I feel that in order to get on, you have to get up and do it. There are loads of chances in hotels for trained staff. The industry had a reputation for employing people without formal qualifications, but not so any more.

'I belong to the Housekeepers' Association, and when I get a chance, I go to their meetings. They are mostly women but I like to think that I contribute. I must be doing ok because I keep getting asked to take work experience students. They get a good training here, although they get very tired cleaning six rooms on their own! I bet they look to my job with envy. It's real management, dealing with staff, resources and budgets. I'm glad I took this route.'

Room maid/attendant

The bedrooms in an hotel are cleaned by the room attendants. Their day may start very early, as in some hotels the maids serve early morning teas. After the guests have departed, either for the day or having checked out, the maids begin their cleaning. The level of cleaning often depends on whether a guest is staying on in the hotel or leaving. This is called a departure. If a guest is to stay on, the attendants have to clean around the guest's belongings, trying not to disturb too much. A departure involves a more thorough cleaning process. This includes making up beds, changing sheets, cleaning the bathrooms, replenishing the soaps and supplying clean towels, emptying the waste bins and generally tidying. Room attendants have the added responsibility of reporting to their supervisor if a guest has not occupied the room. This may be the first sign that the guest has tried to depart without paying and must always be reported. The hours are normally 7.30 am to 3.30 pm. Maids usually work alone, unless they are training a new employee, and will clean on average 12 to 15 rooms each day. In some hotels, there are late-duty maids who clean rooms after late departures. In luxury hotels, they may also turn down the bed covers or change any towels that have been used since the last maid's visit. Maids may also clean the lounge and reception areas as part of their duties.

A room attendant may be qualified with NVQs in house-keeping. There are good opportunities for promotion to floor housekeeper, a supervisory position, assistant head housekeeper and executive housekeeper.

Front office manager

This is a senior management position, which often leads to general management. The front office manager will have had extensive experience in all front office areas including work as a receptionist, shift leader, cashier, reservations clerk and tele-phonist. They will have sales and personnel skills in order to run an efficient team. Most will have NVQs in reception, a GNVQ Advanced, an HND, degree or HCIMA Professional Diploma.

Receptionist

An hotel receptionist will do a variety of jobs depending on the size, location and type of hotel. A receptionist in a small hotel will carry out a range of tasks including reservations, checking guests in and out, taking payments and answering the telephone. A larger hotel will employ staff to perform only one of these duties. They may have a separate reservations department, solely for handling advance bookings. Telepho-nists or switchboard operators are employed to answer and direct calls to various departments. Cashiers specialize in receiving payments from guests, foreign exchange and credit card transactions. Most reception staff work on a shift basis of 'earlies and lates'. An early shift will be from about 7 am to 3 pm and a late shift from 3 pm to 11 pm. There will probably be a handover time of 10 or 15 minutes. Quite often, receptionists will work a late shift and then an early shift, finishing at 11 pm and starting again at 7 am the next day. When completing an early shift, they will not be on duty until the following day at 3 pm.

Promotion in a large hotel is to shift leader, who is responsible for a team of staff for the duration of the shift. From shift leader, promotion is to head receptionist or reception manager, with responsibility for all the shifts for the reception area. Further promotion is to front office manager.

Reception staff should have good personal and social skills, and be well presented. The key skills of communication, and application of number and information technology, are beneficial. Qualifications range from NVQs in reception to GNVQ Advanced courses. Those looking for higher career progression should consider an HND, HCIMA or degree.

Case Study

Kim Lee is a reception shift leader at the Kennedy Hotel in London.

'I started here eight months ago in the reception department. My college was asked by the hotel if they had any suitable reception or reservation trainees. I still had two months to go in college, but my teachers were good and allowed me to finish the assignments over a longer period to allow me to begin the reception job. A typical day was a shift from either 7 am to 3 pm or 3 pm to 11 pm, known as a "late" and an "early". One would normally follow the other, but I preferred the late shift. The two shifts are very different. In the morning, guests are checking out, and on the late shift, they are checking in. We had a computerized system for reservations and reception, which I picked up very quickly.

'The guests come from all over the world and I have met some really nice people. There have also been some awkward guests, and twice there was a bit of a problem in reception. This sometimes happens when we are overbooked and guests are booked out to other hotels. This is done intentionally because some people with reservations don't arrive and overbooking ensures that the hotel is full. The first time you have to tell a guest checking in that the hotel is full is horrible, but as long as the guest knows they are getting the same sort of hotel, or better, and transport, they soon calm down, usually.

'We also exchange currency and take a load of different credit cards. Sometimes it really gets confusing exchanging money from one country to pounds, or the other way around. Balancing the cash register took a long time in the early days.

'Following a two-month training period, I became a receptionist, and then a new computer system was installed. I was good at it and did loads of overtime to train other people. Two weeks ago, I became a shift leader, like a shift supervisor. The next job is reception manager but I think that is a year or two away. In the meantime, I want to work in other hotels for the experience.'

Head porter

The head porter runs a team of porters responsible for the security of room keys, answering guests' queries, giving directions, arranging transport and carrying luggage. They will also deal with left luggage and lost property. In some hotels, they may also be able to make theatre and cinema reservations. The night porter may check in late arrivals, serve snacks and beverages, order newspapers and act as hotel security. Responsible to the front office manager, most are unqualified although many belong to the Société des Clefs d'Or. Many managers and trainees have previous experience with the porters during their training period.

Personnel management

Personnel, in general, is concerned with the recruitment, welfare, training and retention of staff in a company. Employing a department to oversee these functions enables the other departments to concentrate on providing a service. There are three main functions in personnel: administration, recruitment and training. The responsibilities of the personnel manager include keeping employee files, monitoring and controlling staff sickness, job descriptions, contracts, employee benefit schemes, developing training plans and possibly meeting with outside agencies to develop strategies for industry development.

Many personnel managers have specialized personnel qualifications (eg Institute of Personnel and Development), although some have entered the hotel and catering industry as students on a course such as a GNVQ, found they liked it, and then decided to specialize.

Case Study

Geraldine Mullins *is currently on the final year of a Higher National Diploma in Hospitality Management.*

'When I left school at 16, I went to my local college and studied for a GNVQ Advanced in Hospitality. At the same time, I worked part-time in various hotels in the banqueting department, the restaurant and the bars. After the GNVQ, which I passed with merit, I went to a central London college to do an HND. I wish I had found out more about the college before I started there, because I didn't enjoy it and left after only two months. I found a full-time job at a local hotel. They had just recruited a new operations manager, and he saw straight away that I was enthusiastic and hard-working, and I soon became a supervisor. However, I realized that I wouldn't get far in the industry without a Higher National Diploma, so the following September I went to another college and started the course again. This was much more enjoyable. For one placement, I worked in a central London hotel as a receptionist and I enjoyed that very much, even the shift work from 7 am to 3 pm or from 3 pm to 11 pm. Shift work gives me time during the day or evening and the work is changing all the time because of new customers.

'I am studying for an HND but I intend to go on to the final year of a degree. I now also work in a local hotel on reception. It has 50 bedrooms and a bar and restaurant. Once I have qualified, I want to work in a large hotel that has banqueting facilities, and eventually work in conference and banqueting as a manager, or possibly personnel. The good thing is that I don't have to decide just yet what department I want to go in as a career, because the HND covers many different jobs and so I can choose later or even transfer from one department to another.'

Case Study

Four years ago, **Karen Williams** *had just started work as a junior assistant manager at a four-star London hotel, having successfully completed a degree in Hotel and Restaurant Management.*

'Leaving school with four GCSEs and an ambition to work in hotels as a manager in England or maybe abroad, I went to my local college and did a BTEC National Diploma, equivalent to a GNVQ Advanced. While at college, I had three jobs. My first work experience was in the house-keeping department of an hotel. It was hard work and I was only there for two weeks. I learnt all about cleaning rooms, what equipment to use, changing beds and, more importantly, about life in a hotel. For the last two days, I worked with the floor housekeeper, planning rotas and checking rooms. Between the first and second year of the course, I went to work in Germany. Although I had studied the language at college, my language skills improved dramatically. For most of the time I worked in the restaurant and housekeeping. During the last year of the course, I worked in the front office of the hotel. I learnt all about the switchboard, reservations, porter's desk, reception and cashiers.

'I had decided to carry on studying and do a Higher National Diploma in Hospitality Management. During the summer months, between one course and another, I worked in a restaurant kitchen. I had never worked in a kitchen before, apart from collecting the meals for service as a waitress. It was interesting to see how a kitchen worked and, although I decided that I didn't want to work in a kitchen as a chef, the experience of seeing what goes on was invaluable.

'The two-year HND was very interesting. We studied a range of subjects, including business studies, hotel management, human resource management and operational techniques. There were also some optional subjects, and I took conference and leisure facility management, advanced business and languages. I became a student member of the HCIMA when I started the HND and I was able to request information from them. Their magazines often have articles of interest that students can use for assignments. My other source of information was *Caterer and Hotelkeeper*, the weekly magazine. After I completed the HND, I was able to go straight on to the third year of a degree.

'After I left the four-star hotel, I became personnel manager at a three-star hotel next to Euston Station, in the heart of London. I did that for a year and then became conference organizer for a hotel chain. I really enjoyed that, but I missed the personnel aspect of the job. Employment laws are changing all the time and getting back into personnel became a real challenge. Luckily for me, I was offered a job as deputy human resource manager at a new hotel. It is just being built, or rather, refurbished. It was originally an hotel about 100 years ago. Some people might think that going from personnel manager to a deputy is a backward step, but I don't. The hotel is very different; a different size, new challenges, and what is even more exciting is the fact that I am recruiting all the staff for when we open in the autumn of 2000.'

Case Study

A small hotel

*Gerald Hindman is a graduate in the field of hotel and catering manage-
ment, and has spent most of his working life building a career in industrial catering, eventually becoming operations director for Quadrant, the
catering arm of the Post Office.*

In 1991, he realized most caterers' ideal, by purchasing Sutherland
House Hotel, a small luxury country hotel and restaurant on the outskirts
of Deal, a picturesque town in Kent.

The hotel has only five bedroom suites and the restaurant seats
24. The bar is unusual in that guests help themselves from an 'honour'
bar. The restaurant is open to residents and their guests
and sometimes to outside diners, but most business is from small
dinners or luncheon parties and functions – the garden being popular in
summer.

In such an individual and intimate atmosphere, where guests often
become friends, Gerald found himself pivotal to all the activities at
Sutherland House (particularly the cooking), thus ensuring its continued
success and profitability. He has re-modelled and trained a small team of
staff to ensure excellence and the smooth running of the hotel as well as
the comfort and wellbeing of each and every guest.

The staff at Sutherland House consist of an assistant manager and
a housekeeper, who are supported by a part-time chambermaid and
waitress. The gardens are maintained by an outside company, as are
laundry and secretarial services. All staff are totally flexible in their duties
and hours, and working well as a team is essential. Gerald Hindman's
view on working in catering is unequivocal.

'Having managed a very large workforce in the past, I had become
distant from the problems working at the sharp end of the business.
There is little glamour or status attached to our industry, particularly in
the country, which is a great shame as it is a great profession to belong
to. At Sutherland House I am very much involved in all aspects of the
work and have begun to realize the difficulties that staff face.

'The work is basic and often hard and tedious, especially at times of
pressure when there seems almost no time even to draw breath.
However, in the right atmosphere and with a good team spirit, the work
can be almost pleasurable, particularly when the customers are pleasant
and appreciative.

'I have had enormous problems getting the right individuals into the
jobs, and often after training and encouragement, staff have left to go on

to better jobs elsewhere, which is often sad but also very satisfying. The first quality I look for is willingness combined with flexibility. Hopefully, the individual will also be pleasant and definitely have a sense of fun and humour to get through the tough times. I look for good basic common sense and ability to work as a member of a team. After that, I feel that training is essential and formal qualifications desirable to gain the basic cross-section of skills on which to build. Formal training also gives the clearest possible indication that an individual has thought about their career in catering and has opted to study and enter the industry rather than just come into it by accident or for lack of other opportunities. Qualifications, however basic and however obtained, are becoming more and more important, especially when combined with other personal qualities and skills. They allow employees to cope with the demands of this most difficult of service industries and help them to progress as far as they can!'

3 Faster food

Two factors have increased the opportunities for faster food outlets. Firstly, more people have an interest in eating away from home, and it is estimated that within the next two years, half the weekly household food budget will be spent on eating out. Although it may not be possible to spend money regularly on high-class restaurants, people are interested in restaurants with non-expensive, quick-service meals. The second reason is a result of the faster pace of life. Less time, maybe due to work or family commitments, has meant that people choose to eat out rather than cook at home. The fast food industry has seen something of a revolution, driven by the burger, fried chicken and pizza restaurants, which have used their advertising skills to market their products successfully.

The 'faster food' industry can be divided into many categories: restaurants, cafeterias, motorway service stations, snack bars, coffee shops, public houses, takeaway shops, event catering and mobile catering.

Restaurants

Restaurants with specialized menus, using pre-packed, pre-portioned, frozen, chilled or convenience foods are seen on major high streets and retail parks. They have also entered the market at motorway service stations, airports and similar sites nationally and internationally. Many are planning to tender for sites within university and college campuses.

These restaurants include pizza places, fried chicken, burger restaurants, fish and chip shops and steak houses. The emphasis is on providing a quick turnover, suiting both the customer and the restaurant. Staff undergo training on dish preparation, portion control, cash control and selling techniques. They wear a uniform, which clearly identifies them as being part of the restaurant, and have to appear clean and well groomed at all times. Jobs may include frying fish, chicken, or chips, cooking burgers, making pizza toppings, counter service or serving on table, accepting payment, or any aspect of the restaurant activity. This may also include cleaning. Shifts vary according to the establishment and the service offered, but may be very early or late at night. Some restaurants may even be open over the 24-hour period, reducing their menu at quiet times to allow for fewer staff or special cleaning duties of equipment. Perks include meals on duty, free uniforms and laundry. For those working for a group, perks may include the opportunity to transfer, as well as health-care benefits.

Cafeterias

Cafeterias are found in department stores, schools, colleges, universities and motorway service stations. They may have call order bars where light meals can be cooked, or meals may be prepared in bulk and reheated on demand by microwave oven, or kept hot using a bain-marie. This is a cabinet, using dry or wet heat to maintain the temperature of the food. It is usually behind a glass screen for hygiene purposes. Staff are employed either to prepare and cook the food, to serve it as a counter assistant, to accept payment or to clear tables.

Motorway service stations

Motorway service stations provide a 24-hour service for meals, snacks and petrol. Some also have accommodation. The modern trend is for them to be multi-facility with branded names for chicken or burgers, in addition to a self-service cafeteria and a waiter-service restaurant. They provide a selection of hot and cold food and beverages. Alcoholic drinks are not available. The self-service restaurants have a series of areas where customers can choose their food. This could include a soup counter, a salad bar, a hot dish counter, a beverage area and a counter for cutlery and accompaniments. After collecting their food, the customers pay a cashier before sitting down to eat. The food is prepared by qualified chefs and cooks. Counter staff assist customers with the hot dishes, eg steak and mushroom pie with chips and vegetables. Table clearers are employed to clear and clean the restaurant seating area when the customers have finished. Where the customers are served at their table, a bill is presented and the customers pay at a cashier's desk. There are usually smoking and non-smoking areas in all facilities. All staff wear a uniform and may be employed on a three-shift system, to cover the 24-hour period.

Snack bars

Sandwich bars and snack bars are similar to cafeterias, although usually smaller and with no rails or barriers to guide customers. They are often found on high streets, near factories and offices, and in cinemas and theatres. The menu is simple, requiring few staff. In many, the person providing the food takes the money, although if food preparation is involved, a separate cashier should be employed for reasons of food hygiene.

Coffee shops

There are two different styles of coffee shop. American-style coffee shops are found in large hotels, serving snacks, light meals and a choice of beverages. Some, in major cities, operate a 24-hour service. The restaurant layout is usually a series of two- or four-seater tables and possibly a counter area surrounded by stools. Waiter service is for the tables.

Customers pay for their food at a cashier point near the exit. Many hotels use their coffee shop for breakfast service.

The other type of coffee shop is an espresso bar or traditional tea shop with a much smaller menu. The former may be found at main line railway stations and airports, providing a large selection of freshly ground coffees, and pastries. Tea shops provide teas, cakes and light snacks. Examples you may have come across are Starbucks or Costa Coffee.

Public houses

As a result of recent legislation on opening hours and an increase in families choosing to eat out, many public houses now provide substantial food in addition to a fully stocked bar. A public house is run by a publican, who may be the owner or a tenant of one of the breweries. Some breweries employ managers, in which case, the manager is paid a salary and possibly receives a bonus or takes part in a profit-sharing scheme. A tenant rents the public house from the brewery on specific terms agreed by both parties. Some public houses are free houses, that is, they are not tied to a brewery, and the publican can buy supplies from any source. A licence for the provision and consumption of alcohol is awarded by a magistrate, and is only issued to a person who is honest and trustworthy. Even if the public house is a tenancy, it still involves most of the duties of running a small business, including hiring staff, ordering supplies, controlling stocks, bookkeeping and sales techniques. Most public houses are open from about 10.30 am to 11 pm. Some stay open later as they have special licences, and changing legislation will offer many more opportunities as the hours are extended in line with bars in Europe. Staff are employed for all the duties on a full-time or part-time basis. This includes chefs and cooks, waiters, bar persons and cellarmen. Employment is available to both sexes.

Some public houses provide only light snacks, eg sandwiches, salads and pre-cooked pies and pasties. Much of the work can be done by those with an interest in catering, a hygiene qualification, or possibly an NVQ in food service. Other public houses have busy restaurants with a full menu of hot and cold dishes. In these, a chef, qualified with NVQs in food preparation, would be employed. The public house manager may have a GNVQ Advanced, HND or degree.

Many brewery companies run courses for new managers and tenants, ranging from short courses to those lasting several months. These include instruction on drink service, customer care, supplies, legislation and cleaning beer pumps and pipes. Local colleges also offer NVQs in on-licensed premises supervisory management. On- and off-licence courses, offered by many colleges, are essential for those with their own public house or off-licence.

Case Study

Thomas Lawson is manager of The Tavern, a free house in Derbyshire. He completed a BTEC National Diploma in Hotel, Catering and Institutional Operations followed by a degree in Hospitality Management before joining a brewery, quickly becoming an assistant manager.

'My first assistant manager's job was under the guidance of Anne Buxton at The Grosvenor in Manchester. She was an excellent tutor, knowing how to handle the staff and customers to get the best out of them. My training included all the procedures for the brewery, and after about 18 months I was given my own pub, The Crown, in Oldham. It was run down when I first arrived, but I maximized the potential of the pub with the help of a friend of mine, an accomplished actress and singer, who livened the place up at weekends. We also improved our snack service, adding hot snacks to the sandwiches that we had served before. In one of the bars, we introduced a cocktail list, which meant that one bar was ideal for the younger age groups and the other for the traditional pub goers who wanted a drink only. It was almost like running two pubs in one, and turnover increased dramatically. After two years, I went to work abroad and when I returned, I purchased The Tavern.

'The pub had been run really well by a couple, who had decided to move to the coast to buy a small hotel. Most of the crowd were young people who would then move on at closing time to a local club, especially at weekends. When working abroad, I came across the idea of a telephone bar where customers could use phones linked throughout the room. I installed this system in the bar and it soon became very popular.

The bar is still busy five years later. It is hard work but can be very entertaining. Occasionally we have a local singer or band, and we have tried karaoke and talent contests.

'My day starts at around eight in the morning. We often have deliveries then, or I have to stocktake or count floats ready for opening at 11 am. We have a cook every day, who has City and Guilds qualifications. The menu is available all day although most of our food is served at lunchtime and then in the early evening. Sunday lunchtimes are quite good too. We serve a range of hot dishes including favourites like steak pie as well as coq au vin or chicken chasseur. Sandwiches are always available. The rest of the staff are made up of eight part-timers and three full-timers. My wife and I also serve behind the bar. I like to see who the customers are and I wouldn't be able to do that if I sat in an office all day doing paperwork. We all wear a uniform. It's simply a sports shirt with a logo and smart black jeans, but at least we all look the same and can be identified as staff. On a Tuesday and Saturday, I start a bit earlier if I can, in order to clean the pipes. Being a free house, I often get calls from company representatives trying to sell their products, both food and drink. We have tried all sorts but are firmly led by our customers.

'We don't usually have a problem getting people to leave at night, although once or twice we have had to get quite loud with hen nights. They tend to be the loudest and on the phones all the time. When they leave, I finally get to relax for a while. After all day in a pub, my idea of heaven is a sandwich and hot chocolate before bed!'

Takeaway shops

The most common types of takeaway shop are fish and chips shops as well as Chinese, Indian and Greek food. Pizzas, burgers and baked potatoes are also popular in many takeaway shops. Most are open till quite late at night. Food can be ordered in person or over the telephone. Some modern city centre places are offering an e-mail or fax ordering service for office employees. The food is provided in foil containers, boxes or secure wrapping with plastic cutlery or wooden chip forks if needed. Often family run, they employ part-time staff who are mostly counter assistants. Knowledge of food hygiene is essential and a qualification is advantageous.

Elen Macit's *family own Crystal in North London.*

Crystal is a restaurant and takeaway in North London, close to Tottenham Hotspur Football Club, specializing in kebabs and steaks. It was started about 20 years ago by Elen's father, who moved to England from Turkey. Before moving to England, he worked as a waiter in Turkey, and then found employment in a Turkish restaurant in London. After learning about the industry through experience, he successfully applied for a bank loan and opened his own restaurant.

'The busiest days are at weekends, especially when there is a football match on. Takeaways are very popular and we sell a lot of kebabs. The main income is from this side of the business. In the restaurant, steak is one of the popular dishes. There are eight or nine staff working during the busy period; some are full-time and some part-time.

'There are both good and bad sides to the business. Most of our customers are regulars, and over the years they have become more like friends. But it can be very hard work. We have to work long hours, even when the restaurant and takeaway are closed. During the day, we have to buy and prepare the food and clean the restaurant. At weekends, we are open to four in the morning and this is very tiring. It also gets very noisy outside. Sometimes the football crowd are very badly behaved, and at weekends, the local nightclubs allow people to get drunk. This means that the customers may be a problem. Usually, at least once a year, the glass shopfront is broken.

'We have staff that can do many different jobs. They cook, clean, serve at tables, do the takeaways, answer the phone and so much more. Because it's a small family business, everyone helps out and I know all the jobs that have to be done.'

The restaurant is a good business though, and Elen's two brothers plan to take over when they have learnt the business through experience. Elen is going to university, studying to become a hotel or restaurant manager, and she may one day open her own business in the hotel and catering industry, doing something completely different.

Event catering

For the purposes of this chapter, an event is defined as a concert, show or one-off event. Most of the caterers will be owner-operated, similar to a mobile facility, providing hot dogs, ice creams, potatoes and hot chestnuts as well as drinks. The event organizer may allow a contract catering company to be in charge of the catering or allow only certain types of food, thus preventing too many of one type working at the event.

Mobile catering

Most mobile catering units, of which there are several types, are owner-operated. Ice-cream vans may have a secured area or tour the streets, sounding their bell to tempt householders to buy. Burger, hot-dog stalls and other catering vans may be found at football matches, stadiums, race meetings, car-boot sales, agricultural shows and similar outside events. Some have no transport, simply setting up a barbecue area. The advantage of mobile vans is that they can travel to the popular venues, seeking custom. There are several legal issues to consider, especially hygiene and parking regulations. It is not possible simply to set up a table in a busy area. The local authority where you wish to site your catering unit will give advice.

4 Conferences, functions and banqueting

Conferences

A conference can be described as a meeting for consultation, exchange of information and discussion. Some conferences have only a few delegates while others have several hundreds. They may be held on behalf of a political party, to create a new image, launch a new product, communicate to employees or make some kind of public announcement. Venues vary and may include a hotel, dedicated conference venue, college or university campus, sports stadium or even aboard an aircraft, ship or train.

Many hotel companies have their own conference organizers and managers who act as a liaison between the client and the hotel. Opportunities exist in this growing market for conference organizers, many of whom have a hotel and catering background and training to HND or degree level.

The conference organizer is responsible for the sales, planning, administration and operation of conferences. Liaison and good communication with other departments are important. Some conferences require an overnight stay and this will include organizing accommodation and liaising with reservations, reception and housekeeping. Others are at a day rate, from 9 am to 5 pm. Day delegates will need the services of a cloakroom to leave coats and bags, especially in winter. Conferences may also require a registration desk or meeting point. The provision of food and drink will result in the need to communicate with chefs, food and beverage managers and restaurant managers, possibly including planning and arrangements for gala dinners or special diets. Music and entertainment may have to be arranged. Conference requirements for specialized equipment such as lighting, audio-visual equipment, special sets and scenery or a sound system must be met. Delegates may be travelling from abroad and need interpreters or a translation service for the duration of the conference. Badges, information packs, printing, stationery and arrival lists may also be requested. If the conference is for business people, they may require the use of office and secretarial services including word processing, fax, e-mail and travel arrangements.

Each event has its own special requirements and the conference organizer must have a close working relationship with all departments and the client. The hours are often irregular and, when a conference is in progress, may be long and tiring. To be successful, a conference organizer must be able to combine and bring together all the different parts of the business. For those interested in this type of work, which may lead to general management, a degree or HND, and experience, are important.

Functions

A function is the name given to special events for groups of people. This includes weddings, luncheons, cocktail parties and dinner dances. Conferences and banquets are also functions and are usually held inside a purpose-built venue. Here, we shall review the catering procedures for outdoor functions.

Every outdoor catering function is unique, with special requirements and facilities. The organization needs to be planned very well and include every eventuality, as it may not be possible to find extra cutlery, crockery, provisions, equipment or staff at the last minute. It may be that the function will be held in a field or garden, with or without the use of a marquee. The party may be in someone's home, not built or equipped to deal with large-scale catering. In these cases, food may have to be prepared off-site and transported in special refrigerated containers. Alternatively, a temporary kitchen may be set up.

The organizer will need to check the following points:

◆ date required;
◆ type of function, eg wedding or other celebration;
◆ number of people;
◆ layout of site;
◆ availability of cooking, refrigeration and freezing facilities;
◆ utilities, eg gas, electricity, water, telephone and drainage;
◆ washing-up facilities;
◆ staffing needs;
◆ insurance;
◆ alcoholic beverage licence (if required);
◆ transport arrangements for equipment, food and drinks;
◆ toilets;
◆ type of service, eg buffet, restaurant, waiter or self;
◆ tables and chairs;
◆ crockery and cutlery;
◆ service equipment;
◆ rubbish disposal.

The outside catering function needs to be well planned; the successful organizer should have good communication and organizational skills, experience, and a GNVQ Advanced or higher qualification.

Case Study

Stirling Rodger is a senior barman for an outside catering company.

'My job is the service of alcoholic and non-alcoholic beverages, although I have been called upon several times to serve food as well. For large functions, we normally arrive at a venue at about 9 am for a luncheon or afternoon party. If it is going to be an evening function, we normally get there about midday, depending on the numbers involved, the type of venue and facilities.

'When I first arrive I am told where the bar area should be sited. If it is inside a building, I prefer to be away from the kitchen area as this gives me more space and is cooler to work in. Sometimes the host provides all the alcohol and my job is just to serve it. This often limits the choice. Alternatively, the catering company provides the drinks as part of the package. Most of the time we have bottled and canned drinks, although I have set up barrels of beer for a rugby club function. Ice is always a problem. We buy it ready in huge bags and these usually last for the duration. There are usually two of us serving and sometimes it gets very busy, so speed is important. Some parties require just a bar service while others need a wine service too. Usually, we then have an additional assistant to help.

'As the drinks at parties are usually free, we sometimes have a problem with guests who enjoy too much alcohol. I try to get them to drink less, rather than allow them to cause a scene. I'm not tied by measures at celebratory parties, so the guests who are worse for wear may get smaller drinks! Some of the parties are themed and we are requested to dress up to fit the occasion. In the past, I have been comic characters and actors. I usually wear black trousers, white shirt and a tie. The perks of the job are sometimes very good. We are paid quite well, and frequently the host gives me a bottle of champagne to take home. As I have been doing this job for many years, I know all the chefs and owners and have also been given smoked salmon, lobsters and gateaux.'

Banqueting

A banquet is a special function, which could be a breakfast, lunch or dinner for 20 to 1,000 people. Some venues contract out the operation to specialist caterers who are chosen by the client.

In large establishments, all special functions are the responsibility of the banqueting manager and are held in the banqueting suites. The manager organizes staffing, supplies of food and drink, maintenance and costings, and will also meet with clients to design menus to fit their wishes. Many other departments will need to be informed of the function, providing dates, numbers and special requests. Smaller hotels may use multi-purpose rooms together with the expertise of a food and beverage manager or assistant manager. Apart from the organizers and a few chefs and waiters, most banqueting staff are employed on a part-time basis. This includes casual waiters and waitresses, bar staff and cloakroom attendants. A banqueting porter may be employed to move furniture, etc, before the waiting staff lay the tables. Permanent staff may be used to lay up the restaurant with all of the cutlery and equipment, and casual staff arrive prior to the start of the banquet for the service of the meal. If there is a cash bar or the need for a wine waiter, this will usually be the job for a permanent member of staff. Banqueting waiters often work irregular hours, possibly finishing after midnight.

Banqueting managers often have a list of reliable staff who can be called upon to work. They will be experienced, and many are qualified with NVQs or equivalent in food preparation and service.

Case Study

Function and banqueting caterers

Popular function and banqueting rooms can be found in London under the control of proprietor **Joan Crew**. *By converting former office premises, she now has several suites of rooms that can be used singly or in groups depending on the size of the function.*

'During the day, we are very popular with local business and industry. Some of our rooms are used for conferences, seminars and training and although we haven't really tried to develop this corner of the market yet, it appears that this is the direction we are moving in for daytime functions. We offer a wide choice of silver service, plate service, buffet, finger buffet and canapés.

'The staff are a mixture of full- and part-time. Our permanent team includes chefs, waiting staff, porters and bar staff. Some staff work only at lunchtimes, while others work in the evenings. Being flexible, we can offer employment opportunities to many who can only work at certain times. We recruit through word of mouth, colleges, and advertising in the local newspaper, the *London Evening Standard* and *Caterer and Hotelkeeper*. I prefer to employ staff who have a formal qualification, although personality and reliability are just as important, if not more so. Enthusiasm is another quality I look for, as is the ability to work in a team, which I think is crucial in catering. The staff get good perks. Everyone gets fed before a function or banquet begins. I'd hate the idea of someone being so hungry they start licking their lips and drooling at the sight of food. They get paid weekly, depending on the number of hours they work.

'We have a set of menus, which includes choices for each course at varying prices. Anything from £5 to £25 is the usual rate. The customer can choose, on behalf of his guests, dishes such as traditional roasts, lobster, salmon with caper sauce, fillet of lamb with fresh mint or a variety of vegetarian dishes. We purchase our desserts from a supplier who also supplies several luxury hotels. This gives us an excellent choice of quality dishes at reasonable prices and has enabled us to concentrate on other aspects of the business. The wine list is extensive and although we don't have a large cocktail list, it may be something for the future.

'Regular suppliers have often been our life-saver for last-minute changes to numbers expected. We also buy from a local warehouse and have been known to buy one-off items at a local delicatessen.

'As the proprietor, my working hours vary. Catering has provided an interesting and enjoyable life, although at times it gets very tough and is not at all like the soft option that many think. Believe me!'

5 Industrial and contract catering

In 1998, over 1,300 million meals were served in this, the largest employment sector of the catering industry, with over 18,000 outlets. The catering units include:

- business and industry;
- state education;
- public catering;
- independent schools;
- healthcare;
- local authorities;
- Ministry of Defence;
- oil rigs, training centres and construction sites.

The sector can be split into two divisions, historically known as welfare catering and industrial catering.

Industrial catering can be either in-house operations, ie carried out by the business, or provided by a catering contractor. Examples of contract catering companies are Gardner Merchant and Quadrant. As many organizations must now put out to tender for the provision of a catering service, it is often the independent contract caterer who wins the contract. These specialist caterers can be seen in independent schools, colleges and universities, prisons, leisure centres, factories, department stores and airports. The main purpose of the sector is to provide food and drink to people at work, as industry recognizes that better-fed workers provide a larger and higher-quality output.

Welfare catering includes hospitals, schools, forces and prisons, the purpose being the provision of food and drink to those with a social need. Independent contract caterers may also be the providers of the service.

Both sectors work within the constraints of a fixed budget and may be allocated a set amount of money to provide meals. In the industrial sector, the food may be given away to the employees as a perk, or a nominal amount may be charged for each course. The hours vary, for example, in an office or retail park, they may be from 8 am to 4 pm, Monday to Friday. Alternatively, large organizations may employ staff 24 hours a day, seven days each week and require a catering service to operate a similar programme.

Colleges and universities

Compulsory competitive tendering has opened up the college and university market, ensuring that local authorities compete for business with established catering contractors. This is dramatically different from old-style institutional catering where little choice, and poor quality and surroundings, were common. This growing market provides in excess of 37 million meals each year, with some campuses having up to 5,000 customers per day. Consequently they are an attractive market for the contract caterer.

A further factor of the change in the market is the nil subsidy, ensuring that colleges and universities must compete with the high street catering and recognized brand names. Burgers, pizzas, snacks and ethnic foods are now available in surroundings that have changed from the traditional refectory to an attractively furnished environment, using modern equipment and technology. Many contract caterers are introducing their own brands of food, which match those available on the high street, for example, pizzas and burgers. Other campuses have the brand names of Pizza Hut and Burger King, establishing a catering food court similar to airports, and shopping and leisure centres. There is also a demand for traditional meals, especially from those away from home, requiring home-style cooked food, such as roasts and casseroles.

As well as changing the food and furnishings, the staff have modern uniforms, ensuring that a new, fashionable environment is apparent. In-house training in customer care and selling are also available. Opportunities exist for qualified managers, chefs, cooks and counter assistants.

Hospitals

Hospital catering provides food and drink to thousands of patients and staff every day of the year. Most hospitals allow patients to decide for themselves what they want to eat, provided they are not on a restrictive diet. The food is served plated to the patients, often coming already on plates from the hospital kitchens. Alternatively, the food is supplied in bulk, taken to the ward in heated trolleys and plated there. Private hospitals often have a waitress service, similar to that of an hotel.

Hospital caterers make full use of the facilities, equipment and technology, which may include cook-freeze, cook-chill, à la carte service, and vending and counter service, to provide a range of services for patients and employees. Special meals may need to be prepared for those on a special diet, nutrition playing an important part in this sector of the industry.

Catering managers are in charge of a large catering department within a hospital. Their role includes planning menus (with the support of a nutritionist), ordering supplies, and supervisory work during the preparation or service of food.

Opportunities exist for qualified managers, chefs, cooks and kitchen assistants who have NVQs, BTEC National Diplomas, Higher Nationals and degrees. Knowledge of food hygiene is essential. Vacancies are advertised in the newspapers and in *The Hospital Caterers' Association Journal*.

Prisons

Prisoners judge prisons on a variety of factors including visits, letters from home and food. The current thinking is that food should be appetizing and fulfilling, as the inmates are sent to prison as a punishment and not for punishment. As less than £2.50 is spent on meals per prisoner each day, the need to work strictly within a budget is important.

Many kitchens are ill-fitted, using energy-wasteful ovens and equipment, which are unsuitable for the types of dishes being sought. There are currently 37 kitchens scheduled for refurbishment at an average cost of £500,000 each. By providing modern equipment including steamers, deep-fat fryers and heated trolleys, prisons have been able to raise standards.

Much of the fresh produce is produced at prison farms. However, the need to keep to a budget means that other foods have to be purchased from inexpensive sources. This will include manufacturers who have overproduced or are discontinuing a line.

The practice of prisoners being able to tick from a list of choices is currently being introduced. Popular dishes are quiches, lasagne and cod mornay. Old-fashioned metal plates and dishes are being replaced by ceramic tableware. Prisoners are also supplied with their own mugs.

Opportunities exist for qualified chefs, cooks, assistants and catering clerks. For further details, contact the Head of Prison Catering Services, Supply and Transport Division, Crown House, 52 Elizabeth Street, Corby, Northants NN17 1PJ.

School meals

In recent years, local education authorities have made changes in school meal catering. Traditional two-course meals, a main dish and dessert, have been replaced by a cafeteria-style system, giving pupils a choice of dishes. All schools now cater for vegetarians.

The contract for supplying school meals goes out to tender; local authority caterers compete with contract caterers. As in all industrial and contract situations, the need to work within a strict budget is important. Most school meals are prepared on-site, although some are prepared in a central kitchen.

Opportunities exist for supervisors, cooks and counter assistants with NVQs, and at area manager level for those with Higher National Diplomas and degrees. Hygiene qualifications are essential.

Job opportunities

Opportunities exist for managers, chefs, cooks, cashiers, counter-service assistants, waiting staff, catering clerks, storekeepers and porters. Training may be provided by the catering company with in-house schemes and short courses. Applications are always welcome from qualified personnel, who have successfully completed NVQs, BTEC National Diplomas, Higher National Diplomas and degrees.

Case Study

Maureen Haggis *is employed as a catering clerk for a large industrial caterer. She has been there for 12 years, gaining promotion from cashier. There are various grades of staff. In her particular unit, there are catering managers and catering grades one to four. Grade one is given to catering clerks, chefs and cooks with added responsibilities. Other cooks and storekeepers are at grade two. Grade three is for cashiers and grade four is for counter assistants and kitchen porters.*

'Although the unit is open 24 hours each day, five and a half days each week, providing meals, snacks and drinks, I work only from 8 am to 4.30 pm, Monday to Friday.

'My job as a clerk covers many duties. The job description is very broad and I can be asked to act as a supervisor on the counter, do stock-taking, or all the paperwork and invoicing. In the last year I have taken two new qualifications, a food hygiene certificate and a certificate in health and safety practices. These are very important, especially when I am acting as a counter supervisor.

'On a typical day, I will start by counting all the takings from previous shifts and making up floats for the next few shifts, completing all the necessary banking forms. The takings are then collected mid-morning by security. At this point, I begin the rest of the paperwork. This includes completing purchase orders for suppliers, checking delivery notes and invoices and recording entries in the trading account book (TAB). Each month, on a nominated day, we have to stocktake. Together with a storeman and manager, I record the amount of stock we hold. We can then calculate its value. Senior management advise us of our target, a food-cost percentage, and we need to be very close to that figure. If we are not we have to explain why, which may be for an exceptional reason, such as fridge breakdown. To calculate the food-cost percentage, we add together our opening stock and our purchases: the food we have bought. Subtracting the value of the closing stock tells us the value of the stock we have used during a particular month. That figure is divided by the amount of money we have taken to give a percentage. Usually it is around 80 per cent.

'At busy times, usually 11.30 am to 1 pm, I am asked to supervise the counter service. At the end of the lunch service, it is cash handling again, counting the lunch takings.

'For this job you need supervisory skills, the ability to add up and subtract, and have good paperwork systems. If you have all that, the job becomes much easier.'

6 Travel and transport

Airlines

In addition to the core activity of meal preparation for scheduled and charter airlines, the operations incorporate a complex process designed to ensure that both food and equipment are ordered, packed and loaded on to aircraft within precise time frames. Typically, a scheduled Boeing 747 requires in excess of 40,000 items to be loaded, checked and packed into predetermined compartments on the aircraft. Allowing for choice, and dietary and religious requirements, a long-haul flight can be supplied with over 30 different types of meal.

One of the major flight caterers is Alpha Catering Services. They provide 40 million meals, using 33 flight kitchens across three continents. They specialize in providing flight catering services to over 100 airlines, including British Airways, Britannia, Virgin Atlantic and Alitalia. In co-operation with these airlines, appropriate menus are designed and numbers agreed. Bulk food orders are delivered to highly organized kitchens, where the food is then prepared and cooked. Close attention to quality, specification and hygiene control are very important. Many passengers choose an airline based on the quality of the meals served. Specification is important in order to control costs. A leading airline recently removed just one black olive from their individual salads in order to save £65,000 in one year. The prepared meals, together with all associated service equipment, beverages, sundry items, newspapers and duty-free stores, are then assembled on a flight-by-flight basis and loaded on to purpose-built vehicles for transfer to the aircraft. Once on board, they are stored in either the galley, the service area, or in the hold.

On board the aircraft, food and drinks are served by the cabin crew. Using specially designed trolleys they are able to serve a wide choice of beverages and, on many flights, a choice of meals. On some flights there are several meal services. Often there are two or even three classes of passenger: economy, business and first. At the end of the flight, reusable equipment is removed from the aircraft, washed and stored. Leftover food is thrown away. The aircraft is then reloaded to be ready for the next flight.

Opportunities exist for catering managers, chefs, cooks and kitchen assistants. Qualifications for employment with an airline caterer would be similar to those for a restaurant, ie NVQs and GNVQs.

Airports

All airports provide food and beverages to passengers and those collecting travellers. The range of facilities varies according to the demand and size of the airport. They may include silver-service restaurants, snack bars, cafes, coffee shops and licensed bars. Busy international airports will cater for a wide variety of clients with, for example, sushi and oyster bars. Many restaurants and bars are run by a specialist company such as Alpha Airport Catering. In addition, many airports now lease space to branded high street names such as McDonald's, Burger King, Costa Coffee and Garfunkels. Opening times vary according to flight arrival and departure schedules and some may be open all the time to accommodate night flights. There is a wide range of opportunities for those with NVQs and GNVQs in food preparation and service, catering management and beverage service.

Cruise liners

Catering on board ship takes many forms. Luxury cruises are similar to luxury hotels, employing highly-qualified chefs, catering managers and waiting staff. Most of the food is brought on board at the original port and the chefs and catering managers have to work together to plan menus and order food for the duration of the trip. Replenishing stocks may not always be possible. On some cruises, the ship will load seasonal or speciality food from a particular port. The service in the restaurant is highly professional, and is often silver service. Large ships sometimes have several restaurants and the passengers are allocated a particular restaurant for their trip. There may be more than one sitting at each mealtime. Lounge bars and cafeterias may provide snacks between meals. Luxury liners may also have 24-hour room service. Opportunities exist for qualified people to be employed on board ships sailing to areas including the Caribbean and the Mediterranean. The purser, who is in charge of catering, will also be responsible for the licensed bar areas.

Cross-Channel ferries

The more popular ships are those cruising across the Channel. Often they have a number of restaurants and snack bars. Some ships have simple cafeteria-style services while others have a smorgasbord buffet service, which allows the passengers to help themselves. Chefs replenish the buffet table and the waiting staff are employed to organize the restaurant, clear tables and take payments. Shorter crossings mean that the crew have to be highly organized to satisfy all the passengers within a short space of time. A further development has been the Channel tunnel, forcing the cross-Channel ferry companies to be much more competitive. Many of the ships owned by P&O now have silver service restaurants, trying to capture a new market, and are promoting the fact that they now offer a cruise rather than a simple Channel crossing.

Trains

Many trains offer a food and beverage service varying from a dining car to a buffet car or trolley service. The exclusive Orient Express provides accommodation as well as a very high standard of restaurant meals. It employs chefs and waiting staff qualified to the same standard as a high-class restaurant. Buffet cars offer a range of meals, snacks and beverages. Most are pre-prepared and the counter-service staff re-heat meals, serve snacks and prepare beverages. Facilities include microwave ovens, fridges, tea- and coffee-making equipment and a cash register. Before the start of the journey, staff must check their stock and order supplies. During the trip, they need to maintain quality, specifications and hygiene standards. One of the problems for the staff is the train movement, which can make the working conditions difficult. At the end of the trip, they need to reconcile the amount of stock sold with the cash takings. Some trains have a buffet trolley, which is wheeled through the train. This is usually stocked with a range of beverages, sandwiches, cakes and confectionery. Passengers can select from the trolley and have the advantage of being able to stay in their seat.

Other careers in catering

This chapter identifies and explains some of the other opportunities that are available in catering. It may be that you want to combine your interests and learn how to be a cookery writer. Or you may choose to cater for smaller parties in private dining rooms, or in huge amounts as part of the armed forces at events around the world. The suggestions are not exhaustive but offer a range of options for consideration.

Army

Young people are recruited as apprentices aged between 16 and 17½ into the Royal Logistics Corps, where they can train to work in catering. The Army Catering Corps Apprentices College in Aldershot trains people to become soldiers and chefs. When you first arrive at the college, your initial intensive training phase provides you with the skills required by every soldier in the army. Military training is given priority because, no matter how skilled a chef and manager you become as your career progresses, you are always first and foremost a soldier. During the first phase of training, you learn weapon handling, drill, first aid and other soldiering skills. At the same time, you undergo physical training to build up your strength and stamina. After the first few weeks of military instruction, you are introduced to craft training with a range of NVQs, to teach you the necessary skills to become a chef. In addition to learning all about catering for both small and very large numbers of people, you will also learn about cooking under canvas. A Royal Logistics Corps chef is trained to carry out culinary skills in the field, where you have to maintain your own cooking equipment, and may have to manufacture a cooking system so that you can provide meals whatever the conditions. Catering for the army teaches you to be a chef and manager. Computers are used to plan menus and to keep within budget.

Once you have completed your training, you will be posted to wherever the army is serving. This could be in Cyprus, Northern Ireland or the Middle East. Those joining as apprentices serve until they are 18, and then can sign on for a further three years, after which they decide whether to stay in the army or gain a catering position in the civilian world. As your career progresses, you will be given opportunities for promotion and selection for additional training; for example, if you are a corporal and have been selected for promotion to sergeant, you will attend an advancement course that will give you training. To qualify for promotion to sergeant, the soldier will have successfully passed the Education Promotion Certificate. Craft training is given through courses such as the Advanced Cooks Course and the Master Chefs Course. Management training may be given with NVQs and HCIMA qualifications. About 85 per cent of apprentices become warrant officers within the Catering Corps. At this level you will be responsible for feeding perhaps 1,000 people a day in a variety of locations. It may be that you will have a budget of £1 million each year to manage effectively.

For further information, contact your local army careers office.

Royal Air Force

The Catering Trade Group is a major support service within the RAF, providing the complete range of catering services. There are three trades: chefs, steward/mess managers, and catering clerks.

Chefs are employed in the kitchen of an officers', sergeants' or junior ranks' mess. The first two are equivalent to civilian hotels and clubs, and the junior ranks' mess is a large refectory providing multi-choice self-service meals. Some chefs will be employed in hospitals or on flight catering duties. A corporal is often in charge of a kitchen shift on his own and a sergeant or flight sergeant will have overall responsibility for the control of staff and for the food preparation in one of the messes. Warrant officers either serve as assistant catering officers or as the catering officer at a small unit. The work of RAF chefs is similar to that of their civilian counterparts except that, with promotion, the variety of supervisory and management roles can cover a larger field. Trade training at RAF Halton lasts for 15 weeks.

A steward/mess manager is usually responsible for the running of the dining room, bars and reception areas. Some stewards are employed on personal duties in senior officers' residences. Within the messes, junior stewards are employed in the running of the dining room, bars and reception offices, ie similar duties to an hotel. With promotion, the supervisory aspects of their duties increase. A corporal, for example, may be in charge of a department or a mess. Stewards are also employed in RAF transit hotels, which are located at UK terminal airfields. They provide restaurant, bar, reception and room service as well as administrative and accounting systems. Trade training at RAF Halton lasts seven weeks and four days.

Clerk catering is similar to that of a food and beverage controller in the civilian catering profession. Experience is given in stores and stockholding, wholesale and retail food and butchery, food processing and hotel and catering. Training at RAF Halton lasts six weeks.

There are no formal educational qualifications for entry to the Catering Trades Group, although a GCSE grade D or above is advantageous for becoming a clerk. There is, however, a short series of tests. On selection, recruits must complete seven weeks basic training before trade training.

Positions are available for both non-qualified and qualified recruits. Those unqualified are eligible for promotion to senior aircraftman after 12 months and a trade ability test. For promotion to corporal, you need to pass an education test and further training. Qualified entrants join as aircraftmen for steward and chef duties. Those with higher civilian qualifications, for example NVQs levels 2 and 3, and GNVQs, can apply for early promotion.

Extensive opportunities for advancement to officer exist. Positions are also available for entry at officer level for those with degrees and Higher National Diplomas. For further information, contact your local RAF careers information office.

Royal Navy and Royal Marines

To join the Royal Navy as a chef, you need to be aged between 16 and 33. No special educational qualifications are required, although a good general education is essential because the training is demanding. Each entrant has to pass a selection test based on reasoning, numeracy, literacy and mechanical comprehension. You must also have the right qualities for the job, which may include previous experience, physical fitness and the ability to learn and take orders.

Royal Navy ships can be found in all corners of the world and there are many shore bases in the UK and abroad. Wherever people are serving, they have to be fed, and the chefs have to provide food of the highest standard. They may also have to prepare banquets, large cocktail parties, lunch and dinner parties.

The first part of training is at 'HMS Raleigh', a modern shore establishment in Cornwall. For eight weeks, you will learn about marching, wearing uniforms, naval traditions, team skills, firefighting, security and weapon handling. The next 15 weeks make up your professional training at HMS Raleigh, within the Royal Navy Supply School. Training is divided into three sections. The first four weeks cover ordering, issuing, stocktaking and control of provisions. Over the next nine weeks, there are practical and theoretical cookery classes, which lead to NVQ levels 1 and 2. During this phase, you will be trained to a basic food hygiene standard. Skills learnt include preparation of stocks and sauces, fish and meat dishes, vegetables and salads, desserts and baking. The third and final section lasts two weeks and includes practical galley experience, field cookery and firefighting training. Each section of the course has an examination and practical assessment. Those completing their training successfully will be drafted into a fully active catering department. At this stage, chefs can consolidate their skills and gain experience. Work opportunities range from feeding up to 1,200 people on an aircraft carrier or working within the confines of a submarine. Those with excellent skills may represent the Royal Navy in cookery competitions nationally and compete against civilians.

Stewards, both men and women, act as serving staff on shore establishments. On board ship, they serve food as well as drink in the wardroom. After basic training, to learn food-service skills they spend a further period learning about wines and the duties of a wine steward. Those successful will gain an NVQ in food and drink service.

The Royal Marines, as part of the Royal Navy, undergo the same catering course at the RN cookery school, HMS Raleigh, as those in the Navy. The main difference is that chefs in the Marines must complete the 30-week Royal Marine commando course prior to specializing as chefs. They may, and often are, called upon to fulfil an active service combat role in the event of an emergency or whenever required to do so. The commando course is carried out at the training centre in Devon and those that are successful are awarded their green beret. Once a fully-fledged marine, there are annual tests for fitness and weapon skills. As chefs, their duties may have to be performed in battle conditions, at extremes of temperature, in field conditions, in the main galley of a ship or at formal dinners in the officers' mess. Full training is given and the qualifications, NVQs, can be used in later civilian life. Promotion prospects are excellent. For further information contact your local Royal Navy careers office.

Cake design

Special occasions are nearly always celebrated with a cake, from a gateaux to a formal iced masterpiece. There are a number of qualifications for different examining bodies and your local college or adult education centre will be able to guide you within this specialization. Historically, some cake decorators worked from home, providing patisseries with cakes for special occasions. Alternatively, they were employed in a bakery producing cleverly piped work in royal icing, often with non–edible adornments. Over the last two decades, specialists have brought new horizons to the art of cake decorating. The Australian soft-icing style can be seen at many a celebration, with most beautiful hand-crafted flowers made from icing.

Case Study

Pat O'Neill *is a lecturer in cake decorating and design and in food preparation and cookery.*

'It was in my last year at technical school that I first fell in love with royal icing, proudly making a Christmas cake. Next came my sister's 21st birthday cake, copied to the best of my ability from a magazine. It was royal-iced with rosebuds and forget-me-nots. By the time it was my best friend's and my own 21st, I had progressed to an Australian book and shaped bases, still working with royal icing. Over the next 16 years, I progressed, making many family celebration cakes, from christenings to weddings.

'Then one magical day, I found that the postman's wife taught classes in adult education. After seeing some of my work, she allowed me to start in the second year. It was the third term before I really mastered the true way of coating a cake with my beloved royal icing. There was no stopping me as I entered local competitions and then enrolled for a two-year part-time course at the local bakery college. It was a design and decorating course, which also included heraldry. I proudly passed with three distinctions.

'Looking back, it is hard to say what creation gave me the greatest thrill. Three stand out in my mind. My 21st was shaped as a cushion with piped flowers, all self-taught. A four-tiered wedding cake had the top edge of each tier finished with tiny piped rosebuds, including the celebration cut (cut out and wrapped in ribbon with a bow to make the cake easy for the couple to cut). This was made for the nephew of the hotel owner where my son worked. The cake stood on a deep silver cake stand that had been used for Prince Charles's christening cake. Most recent was for a colleague who had baked her daughter's wedding cake and had it decorated by someone who had no idea of royal icing. In a week from a disaster I managed to strip the three tiers and turn them into a beautiful royal-iced cake fit for the very important wedding. The cake was for a couple in the services and was to be cut with a ceremonial sword!

'Less interesting to me are the design and production of children's novelty sponge cakes, which take so much time and have to be completed at the last minute to remain fresh.

'If you decide that you want to make cakes for sale from home, you must comply with the new hygiene regulations. You must register with the local Environmental Health Office, which will carry out safe hygiene checks and continually monitor your facilities. If you decide to be employed as a cake decorator, opportunities also exist in local bakeries and specialist shops.'

Hotel and restaurant inspector

When hotels and restaurants are given a star rating, it is as a result of being inspected for quality and/or facilities. Inspectors, all who have a great deal of industry experience, are employed by organizations such as RAC, AA or Michelin to assess the service provided. It is not such an easy job as many people imagine. The role includes travelling the country to various establishments. Once there, they have to judge a range of dishes and wines as well as the quality, in the case of an hotel, of all departments the guest may use. A typical inspection may mean sampling a range of dishes, using room service, the leisure facilities and making additional requests on the hotel such as extra towels. As each inspection is usually only one night, or one meal, the inspectors have to quickly prepare a detailed report before moving on to the next destination, so are always under pressure.

Cookery editors and journalists

Publishers of cookery books and magazines recruit staff who have writing skills and an interest in cookery, as well as using freelances. Some may be trained chefs or cooks. They may have to research and write articles on different types and styles of cookery, ingredients, methods, cookery competitions and possibly suitable wines to complement a meal.

Directors' dining rooms

Directors' dining rooms can be found in private merchant banks and major corporations. The idea is to facilitate a dining service for upper management and their guests, in order to discuss business in private and confidential surroundings.

The voluntary sector

Most of the careers we have looked at so far have been in either the private or the public sector. Growing opportunities exist in a third sector, the voluntary sector, which provides food, drink and sometimes accommodation to those in need. Through fund-raising activities, charities assemble the necessary provisions and may have a small team of paid staff who co-ordinate and work with unpaid volunteers. You may have heard of such voluntary organizations already, for example, soup kitchens from churches and the YMCA who each day feed people in need, providing them with healthy, nutritionally balanced food. Although run by volunteers, they are still bound by the law. An important aspect to this is food hygiene training, which is essential for those undertaking practical duties in the service and preparation of food.

Case Study

Andrew Jenkins *set up the catering facility at the FACTS centre, a specialist medical and resource unit for people with HIV infection. The cafe opened in 1993 and its main focus was not the menu or type of service, but the idea that eating together could provide a social focus for the regular and quickly expanding client group. FACTS has charitable status and has always employed volunteer workers.*

'I successfully completed a BTEC National Diploma in Hotel and Catering (equivalent to a GNVQ Advanced), especially for vegetarians, at Plymouth College of Further Education. While there, I worked part-time at Cranks, the vegetarian restaurant group. On leaving college, I was employed there on a full-time basis as a manager, completing various in-house training programmes.

'After five years as a restaurant manager in the West End of London, it was a refreshing challenge to be offered a position to build up a completely new service with a volunteer group of mixed ability, offering subsidized meals. The main difference has been the motivation of staff – someone working casually in a busy West End restaurant expects a decent wage, whereas I am now dealing with people who actually wanted to offer their services and experiences for their own personal reasons with no wage. This generally means that volunteer workers are keen to offer their time, are reliable and interested in their work. However, the other side of the coin shows some workers who use the excuse "I'm just a volunteer" to avoid taking the role seriously. In my experience, you have similar problems with paid and unpaid workers – some are poor timekeepers, others not interested in learning new skills and some are difficult to work with. If I encounter a problem with one of the volunteers, I try to deal with it in the same way as I would with a paid member of staff, by remembering that the clients using the centre expect and deserve to be treated as any other paying customer.

'The next step was to take unpaid employment as seriously as paid, providing a recruitment process, interview, job description and assessment. This important change enabled me to build a strong group of committed volunteers who were happy to organize and run the cafe service, giving me the time to look at franchising the services to other centres. All staff have completed a one-day essential food hygiene course, which looks at food poisoning, bacteria, equipment, pests legislation and kitchen organization. Many have also completed customer awareness courses.

'Our menus initially were wholefoods, a result of my interests and previous employment. Client-led demand changed this to a home-style, English cookery, which has proved to be a huge success. Due to the nature of the illness, our menus are not normally spicy or high in fibre but, apart from that, are well-balanced, healthy meals.

'Some people ask why we don't employ a full-time chef to run the service. Simply, he or she would not have time to socialize with the clients, ask how they are, direct them to other services and prepare the occasional specialist meal. Volunteers do, and by their nature, care about the client group they are serving. Why else would they be here?'

Qualifications and attributes for the voluntary sector

In general terms, catering in the voluntary sector is little different from the private or public sectors (see previous chapters). The processes of ordering supplies, compiling menus, arranging staff duties and abiding by the laws, together with food preparation and service, are no different from many profit-making organizations. The two additional considerations are the volunteer workforce and the special needs of the customers.

8 Top tips for getting into the industry

Employing the right strategy can make all the difference to your success in applying for jobs. There are various publications and agencies, which are particularly important for people looking for hotel and catering work, including the weekly *Caterer and Hotelkeeper*. Many people enter the industry for the first time as part of their work experience from a college course or a part-time job. This is a useful introduction, as you will be able to glean a variety of experiences before making choices on where you would like to work and begin your full-time career.

Applying for jobs, filling in application forms and going for interviews can be tedious and depressing, but you must work hard at job hunting in order to succeed.

Letter of application

♦ Do a rough draft of the letter to make sure that you have covered all the essential points.
♦ Provide details of your qualifications and experience on a separate sheet (see curriculum vitae below).
♦ Make sure that there are no spelling mistakes or grammatical errors in your letter. If you are not sure, ask someone to read it for you, and use a dictionary.
♦ Use good-quality paper that is not torn or creased.

- Keep your letter brief and concise, and mention where you saw the advert.
- Keep a copy for reference.

Curriculum Vitae

Make sure it is up to date and provides details of all your qualifications and experience.

The interview

For most jobs within the hospitality industry, your appearance, manner and general acceptability will be as important as your practical skills.

The right things to say and do

- Be on time for the interview.
- Make sure you are well groomed with tidy hair, clean shoes and hands.
- Be lively and confident.
- Dress neatly.
- Smile and keep eye contact with the interviewer.
- Speak clearly, without mumbling, and avoid 'you know' or 'sort of'.
- Be honest, but try to sell yourself to the employer. Try to impress by telling them your good points and how you could be of use to them.
- Don't allow yourself to get angry or irritated. The interviewer may be testing your ability to work under stress, or with angry or tired guests.
- Give full answers rather than 'yes' or 'no', but try not to ramble.
- Appear interested in the job.

The wrong things to say and do

- Don't be over-confident or aggressive.

- Don't smoke.
- Don't giggle or be silly.
- Don't chew gum.

You will find interviews less frightening if you prepare well for them. The interviewer is sure to ask some questions, and if you are prepared, you will appear more confident and relaxed. For example:

- 'Why do you want to work in catering/hotels?'
- 'Do you cook at home?'
- 'Do you have a part-time job?'
- 'If so, what is involved and what are you responsible for?'
- 'If you have a full-time job, why do you want to leave?'
- 'Where do you see yourself in five years' time?'
- 'Why do you want to work for (name of company)?'
- 'What do you know about this company?'
- 'What skills do you have that you think will be good for this job?'
- 'Do you have any hobbies or interests?'
- 'Tell me about your family.'

They may ask a few technical questions regarding the job you have applied for. For example:

'Plan a menu for four people.'

Don't simply answer the question, but ask for the boundaries, such as, 'How much can I spend?', 'What season of the year?', 'Are there any favourite dishes for the guests?', 'Any allergies?'. Try to impress them with your thought processes.

Prepared questions show the interviewer that you are keen and interested. Try to ask at least one question, which should be sensible, but if you really can't think of anything, just say that you feel all the points you had thought of have been dealt with. Example questions are:

- 'What are the opportunities for promotion?'

♦ 'Is the company looking to expand?'
♦ 'Are there any opportunities for further training?'

Saying 'thank you'

As soon as you have had your interview, you may help your prospects by writing a thank-you letter to the interviewer. First, it will act as a reminder of who you are and what skills you have to offer. Second, if you were unsuccessful, there may be other opportunities more suited to your skills within the company and the letter may work in your favour. Third, you can use the letter to reinforce something brought up during the interview or something you forgot to mention. Finally, it is seen as polite and courteous to thank someone for their time.

Accepting the job and starting work

If you are offered the job, make sure you understand fully what is expected of you before you commit yourself. Make sure that you realize the rates of pay, hours, shift times, holiday entitlements and methods of pay. It is no good saying after your first week that you thought you were being paid £4.15 per hour when it is only £3.20. Or you were being paid monthly instead of weekly. Or 44 hours each week instead of 38. Or two weeks holiday instead of three. If you have any doubts or queries, now is the time to clear them up and make your position absolutely clear. Only write a letter of acceptance when you are fully aware of all the terms and conditions, and at that stage you are in a position to sign a contract of employment.

9 The future of the industry

The hospitality industry provides full- and part-time employment to over two million people, and the job-creating potential is greater than many other industries. It is estimated that at any one time there are 100,000 job vacancies, and one in five of every new jobs created nationally is in catering, hotel administration, and management. Opportunities in the future will come from a wide range of new ventures.

Budget hotels

Recent years have seen an enormous growth in the budget hotel market, with new hotels being launched on a weekly basis. This type of budget hotel is very successful in Europe, and increasingly in the UK. Groups such as Travel Inn, Travel Lodge, Ibis or Holiday Inn Express offer value for money accommodation and usually have a restaurant nearby as part of the complex. Guests pay on arrival and because there are no extra costs, such as room service or telephones in the rooms, they simply return the key without needing a formal checking-out process. Many of the staff employed have transferable skills, and you will often see them in various departments of the hotel. They might have skills in reception, restaurant and housekeeping. Because this is an expanding sector within the industry, there are many opportunities for promotion.

Public houses

There are two developments in public house management. Firstly, anticipated changes in licensing laws will increase the hours that pubs and clubs are open, so generating more job opportunities. Secondly, pubs are becoming more family focused, many with restaurants or garden areas for families to enjoy.

Information technology

The industry has already seen reservations made over the Internet, or goods and services delivered directly to your home. As more and more people become accustomed to technological advances and are able to access the services, so the industry will develop. Notwithstanding the fact that the industry is service orientated with a high demand for people, IT will be used to provide a better and more efficient service and may be used to reduce some of the more menial tasks. This doesn't mean that there will be fewer jobs, but many more opportunities for individuals with hospitality skills and an all round education including communication, numeracy and IT will become available.

Disposable income

Eating out can be a costly experience and not one that many people can have regularly. However an increase in family-type restaurants such as Beefeater or Harvester, or local pubs doing food, enables more people to dine out without too much expense. It is estimated that in the next decade, over half of a person's food budget will be spent on eating out. This in itself will create more job opportunities for trained staff.

10 Qualifications available

There are various training routes for people entering the industry. Many people aged 16+ choose to go to a college of further education in order to gain a relevant qualification before starting their career, some train on a part-time basis attending college weekly, and others seek employment with a company offering an in-house training scheme. The following section details training opportunities. They are not in any particular order, as the industry allows for employees to have a wide range of qualifications. Not all hotel managers will have degrees. Not all supervisors will have a GNVQ Advanced in Hospitality and Catering. In general terms, NVQs at levels 1 and 2 are craft-orientated, whereas at level 3, they are supervisory; GNVQs lead to a more administrative or sometimes a supervisory position; Higher National Diplomas and degrees lead to supervisory and management positions.

Most colleges offer their own packages made up of a series of qualifications. It may be that while studying for a GNVQ programme in hospitality and catering, you will also study for some NVQs. Completing unit two, Food and Drink Operations, or option unit eight, Providing Food Preparation and Cooking, on the GNVQ Advanced programme for example, may in some colleges complement an NVQ in food preparation. Students may also study for complementary courses including wines and spirits, nutrition and food hygiene as part of their programme of study. These subjects may be integrated into, for example, a GNVQ timetable or be separate units.

Training in Scotland

In Scotland, the courses are similar but the names are slightly different. A GNVQ is a GSVQ, NVQs are SVQs, and National Diplomas are SCOTVEC, which stands for Scottish Vocational Education Council.

General National Vocational Qualifications

General National Vocational Qualifications (GNVQs) are currently awarded at three levels: Foundation, Intermediate and Advanced. They have been designed to provide a broad educational base, leading to employment in the hospitality and catering industry. Qualifications are awarded by City and Guilds, Edexcel/BTEC and RSA. They use the same specifications and so are equivalent in content and level. Colleges decide which examining body to use. They may opt for City and Guilds for NVQs and Edexcel/BTEC for GNVQs or vice versa. Or it may be that some levels are assessed by one awarding body and some by another. There are no hard and fast rules; the college decides.

GNVQ assessment is made through a combination of internal and external requirements. This means that students have to keep a portfolio that is assessed, as well as sitting some tests or externally-set work. Generally, one third of the overall assessment will be externally set and marked by the awarding bodies.

GNVQ Foundation in Hospitality and Catering

The Foundation level in hospitality and catering is a very basic introduction to the industry for those people with few or no academic qualifications. To be successful, you must complete three mandatory units and three optional units. The optional units are chosen by the college from a list given in the qualification specifications. They are optional to the college but not necessarily to the student.

The mandatory units are:

◆ *Unit one* – Exploring Hospitality and Catering (Foundation);
◆ *Unit two* – Exploring Food and Drink (Foundation);
◆ *Unit three* – Exploring Accommodation and Reception (Foundation).

The optional units are:

◆ *Unit four* – Exploring Customer Service;
◆ *Unit five* – Health, Safety and Food Hygiene;
◆ *Unit six* – Exploring Restaurants from Different Countries;
◆ *Unit seven* – Planning Diets;
◆ *Unit eight* – Working as Part of a Team;
◆ *Unit nine* – Preparing for Employment.

GNVQ Intermediate in Hospitality and Catering

The Intermediate course is for students with GCSEs at grades D and E. A student will normally be at least 16 years old. Generally, it is a one-year full-time course and most aspire to progress to the Advanced programme. To be successful, you must complete three compulsory units and three optional units. A GNVQ Intermediate is broadly equivalent to GCSEs at grades A–C.

The compulsory units are:

◆ *Unit one* – Investigating Hospitality and Catering;
◆ *Unit two* – Investigating Food and Drink;
◆ *Unit three* – Investigating Accommodation and Front Office.

The optional units are chosen from:

◆ *Unit four* – Investigating Customer Service;
◆ *Unit five* – Basic Costing in Hospitality and Catering;

- *Unit six* – Preparing for Employment in Hospitality and Catering;
- *Unit seven* – Promotional Activities in Hospitality and Catering;
- *Unit eight* – Food Hygiene;
- *Unit nine* – Food, Nutrition and Diet;
- *Unit ten* – Purchasing and Quality Control.

GNVQ Advanced in Hospitality and Catering

The Advanced level, also known as the vocational A level, is for students with GCSEs at grades A–C, or an Intermediate level GNVQ or equivalent. The GCSEs do not usually have to be in any particular subject, although a good all-round education is preferred, including maths and English. Students should be at least 16 years old. The course is usually two years in duration and may include some links with industry, for example, work experience. In order to complete this course, students need to pass six compulsory units and six optional units. Additional units may be available to complement the course and, although not essential, enhance the students' learning and so are looked upon favourably by employers and universities. Those who are successful may progress to employment within the industry, leading to a supervisory role, or towards higher education as entry on to a Higher National Diploma programme or degree. Employment opportunities are available in hotels, catering companies, airlines, restaurants, cruise ships, institutional catering and leisure centres. Jobs include floor housekeeper, catering officer, hotel receptionist, restaurant supervisor and cabin crew.

The compulsory units are:

- *Unit one* – The Hospitality and Catering Industry;
- *Unit two* – Food and Drink Operations;
- *Unit three* – Accommodation and Front Office Operations;
- *Unit four* – Customer Service;
- *Unit five* – Safety, Security and the Environment;
- *Unit six* – Purchasing, Costing and Control.

The optional units are:

- *Unit seven* – Providing Food and Drink Services;
- *Unit eight* – Providing Food Preparation and Cooking;
- *Unit nine* – On-Licensed Operations in Hospitality and Catering;
- *Unit ten* – Providing Accommodation Service;
- *Unit eleven* – Facilities Operation;
- *Unit twelve* – Providing Front Office Services;
- *Unit thirteen* – Front Office Administration;
- *Unit fourteen* – Hospitality Business Operations;
- *Unit fifteen* – Event Supervision in Hospitality;
- *Unit sixteen* – Hospitality in the Tourism and Leisure Industry;
- *Unit seventeen* – International Hospitality;
- *Unit eighteen* – Marketing for the Hotel and Catering Industry;
- *Unit nineteen* – Human Resources in Hotel and Catering;
- *Unit twenty* – Personnel and Training for Hotel and Catering;
- *Unit twenty-one* – Career Development in Hotel and Catering.

Alternative GNVQs

In addition to a GNVQ in hospitality and catering, it may also be possible to enter catering, hotel administration and management with a GNVQ in leisure and/or tourism. These are also awarded at Advanced, Intermediate and Foundation level.

An Advanced GNVQ in Travel and Tourism includes the following compulsory units:

- Investigating Travel and Tourism;
- Customer Service in Travel and Tourism;
- Worldwide Travel Destinations;
- Marketing Travel and Tourism;
- Tourism Development;
- Travel and Tourism in Action.

An Advanced GNVQ in Leisure and Recreation includes the following compulsory units:

◆ Investigating Leisure and Recreation;
◆ Customer Service in Leisure and Recreation;
◆ Safe Working Practices in the Leisure and Recreation Industry;
◆ Marketing in Leisure and Recreation;
◆ The Sports Industry;
◆ Leisure and Recreation in Action.

At Intermediate and Foundation level, the GNVQ combines Leisure and Tourism and includes compulsory units of Investigating, Marketing and Customer Service within the Leisure and Tourism Industry.

National Vocational Qualifications

National Vocational Qualifications (NVQs) have now been recognized within the industry for several years, and are available at different levels. Level 1 indicates the ability to perform basic or routine tasks, which provide the broad foundation of progression. Level 2 recognizes competence in a more demanding range of activities, which require a degree of individual responsibility. Level 3 denotes skilled work of a complex nature and the ability to undertake a supervisory role. Level 4 demands specialist or technical expertise and the ability to undertake professional work.

NVQs are based on workplace assessments. When a course is run at a college, the assessments are carried out in conditions that closely match a workplace situation. This is known as a Realistic Working Environment (RWE). It may be that the college has a training restaurant or kitchen. Alternatively, some assessments may be made when a student is on a work experience programme. The qualifications are offered by a number of awarding bodies including City and Guilds of London Institute (C and G) and Edexcel/BTEC. If you attend a course within a college, it is likely that you will be assessed and graduate with a certificate from either of these two organizations.

There are no entry qualifications for NVQs, and you don't always have to begin at level 1. General education, previous qualifications and experience may enable you to begin at a higher level. Also, there are no timescales, so candidates can take the assessments as and when they are ready if it is convenient for the assessor.

The qualifications are recognized by many European countries, as they are similar, using industry-based levels of competence. This gives qualified people the opportunity to travel.

NVQ level 1 in Catering and Hospitality may be gained in the following:

- Reception;
- Porter Service;
- Housekeeping;
- Guest Services;
- Food and Drink Service;
- Kitchen Portering;
- Preparing and Serving Food;
- Serving Food and Drink;
- Food Preparation and Cooking (General).

Level 2 includes:

- Bar Service;
- Reception;
- Housekeeping;
- Hospitality Service;
- Hospitality Quick Service;
- Food and Drink Service;
- Food Preparation and Cooking;
- Residential Service.

Level 3 includes:

- Kitchen and Larder;
- General;
- Patisserie and Confectionery.

Modern apprenticeships

A modern apprenticeship is a work-based training programme with a range of vocational and key skills in a specific area. Modern apprenticeships are available for chefs, restaurant management, accommodation managers, and for those who work in fast food. They are currently being developed for those wishing to work in food and drink. There is no fixed time frame, although it is likely that it will take between two and three years to reach NVQ level 3, combining specialist skills with NVQ key skills. The employer undertakes to pay an appropriate salary, provide reasonable experience and employ the trainee with a view to permanent employment after training. The trainees pledge to work to the best of their ability and work hard in order to achieve their training plan. Modern apprenticeships are designed for those who want practical work rather than staying on at school or college. Those who are successful will be awarded a Certificate of Modern Apprenticeship from the Hospitality Training Foundation.

National traineeships

Similar to a modern apprenticeship, this takes about two years to complete and leads to a qualification at level 2.

BTEC Higher National courses in hotel and catering

BTEC Higher National courses are available to those who have successfully completed a GNVQ Advanced course, A levels or an equivalent qualification. The A levels and GCSEs do not have to be in any particular subjects, although maths and English are beneficial for future career prospects. Students are normally at least 18 years old.

There are many programmes offering different units, but they all enable those who are successful to begin a career at supervisory and junior management level. Most of the courses have several periods of work experience over the two or three years. As some students will have progressed from A levels and others from hospitality vocational courses, some colleges offer a short conversion course for those with little or no experience within the industry. Assessments are in the form of detailed assignments, practical assessments, case studies, business plans, strategies and possibly examinations. Some Higher National courses are linked to a university, which runs a degree programme. Those achieving very high grades on an HND may be allowed to transfer to the final year of a degree.

Hotel, Catering and International Management Association

THE HCIMA is the professional association for managers and international managers within the hospitality industry. It is also an internationally accredited examination and awarding body, and offers two programmes of study, leading to either the Professional Certificate or Diploma for managers in the industry. Designed to meet industry needs, these flexible study programmes are offered as modular courses in over 60 colleges in the UK. Students have the option to study part-time, by block release, distance learning and, exceptionally, full-time.

Professional Certificate

Enrolment on to the HCIMA Professional Certificate is limited to those who are currently employed within the industry in full-time employment, or who have in the past worked for at least two years within the industry, preferably at supervisory level. Additionally, students should either have appropriate NVQs, four GCSEs at grades A–C, or sound experience together with a GNVQ Intermediate or equivalent.

Professional Diploma

To be eligible to enrol for the Professional Diploma, students must either be working in the industry in a supervisory position or have worked for at least one year in the industry and have completed the Professional Certificate. Additional entry qualifications may be acceptable, including lengthy experience or NVQs, BTEC National Diplomas or GNVQs.

Degrees and Masters programmes

Degrees are offered in a number of hotel, catering and food-related subjects. Degree courses require at least two A levels or H grades, or a GNVQ or equivalent with exceptional grades, and students should be over the age of 18. Courses vary from three to four years but in some cases may be less if the student has other qualifications, for example, a degree in a subject not related to catering. Many programmes incorporate lengthy work experience placements, usually with payment. Most universities expect degree students to have GCSE grades A–C in English and maths. A European language is advantageous. It is advisable to have some work experience in the hospitality and catering industry before applying for a university course.

Masters programmes are best suited to those who have completed a first degree or equivalent, together with employment at supervisory or management level. Most postgraduate courses are on a part-time basis due to the majority of students being employed. Masters programmes are available in hospitality management, international hotel management, tourism, hotel and catering management and business administration.

British Institute of Innkeeping

The Institute have three courses in:

◆ catering management;
◆ financial management;
◆ business development.

Each of the above courses consists of 18 hours trainer contact time. Additionally, candidates must complete a detailed case study and written examinations.

Other short courses offered by the British Institute of Innkeeping include Licensed Public House Management (three days) and National Licensee's Certificate Course (one day).

Further information can be obtained from the British Institute of Innkeeping.

The Royal Institute of Public Health and Hygiene

Most of the courses can be followed on a part-time basis, and complement an additional programme of study. For further information, apply to the Royal Institute of Public Health and Hygiene.

Primary Certificate

The Primary Certificate in Food Hygiene is recognized as the necessary standard for food handlers of high-risk foods, and the syllabus has been designed so that students can undertake it as an integral part of a wider range of study. The course, of six hours duration, covers the essentials of food hygiene, including food poisoning, bacteria, pest control and legislation. It is taught at many further education colleges and in-house at many catering and hotel establishments.

Certificate in Food Hygiene

This is a theoretical course for those working with food and dealing with staff at a supervisory level. It provides a thorough understanding of all important aspects of food hygiene, including up-to-date legislation. The course is usually held over approximately 24 hours with an external examination at the end. Subjects covered include various types of bacteria, food poisoning, food premises and equipment, food preservation, the role of the Environmental Health Officer, and legislation. The course is examined by a two-hour written paper.

Diploma in Food Hygiene, Advanced Level

This is a theoretical course for those managing a food business, and who have successfully completed the Certificate level. It provides an in-depth understanding of all the issues relating to hygiene, including current legislation. Subjects covered include those on the Certificate course together with quality control, dairy products, cleaning and disinfection, mass catering, meat and meat products, fish and fish products, bakery products and education of food handlers. An Environmental Health Officer puts a significant amount of input into the course. The course is examined using two two-hour written examinations and an oral examination. Those completing the Diploma may qualify as members of the Institute (MRIPHH).

Certificate in Nutrition and Health

This part-time course is designed for people interested in the practical application of nutrition and healthy eating. It highlights the effect of food on health and can assist in basic menu-planning skills.

Royal Society of Health

The Royal Society sets standards, and moderates examinations for a wide variety of nutrition and health issues. The courses are often used to complement a wider educational programme, although they can be taken individually. Courses include:

◆ Diploma in Nutrition;
◆ Certificate in Nutrition;
◆ Certificate in Essential Food Hygiene;
◆ Diploma in Food Hygiene Management;
◆ Certificate in Food Retailing.

Wine and Spirit Education Trust Ltd

Certificate course

The Certificate programme is designed as an introductory-level qualification, intended for those with little or no previous knowledge of wines, spirits and other alcoholic beverages. Successful candidates will be able to interpret alcoholic beverage labels, describe tasting sessions and give basic advice on choice, service and responsible consumption of alcoholic drinks. Areas included are history, wines from around the world and various spirits. The duration of the course will vary in each establishment, but most are two hours each week for 10–12 weeks, culminating in an external examination.

Higher Certificate

This course is designed to provide knowledge of a wide range of wines, spirits and liqueurs. Successful candidates will be able to describe the characteristics of the principal wines and spirits of the world and name the key factors influencing those features. As a result, they will be in a position to advise management, answer customer enquiries and make informed selections of wines and spirits in a variety of situations. The 30-hour course also covers legal aspects. There is an examination at the end of the course.

Diploma Course

For those who have passed the Higher Certificate, there is a two-year Diploma programme. The in-depth course is organized into two parts, each held from January to May with an examination in June. Successful candidates will have completed parts A and B. Current fees are £550 per part for tuition at the Trust and £220 per part for studying at home.

For further information on all the courses offered, contact the Wine and Spirit Education Trust Ltd.

11 Hospitality college courses

There are many different colleges and different courses in the country. Normally, school-leavers are encouraged to go to their local college, although courses may vary from one to another. It is important to check with several colleges for the range of courses included within the package. For example, a GNVQ Advanced course in hospitality and catering may differ from one college to another, simply because of the optional and additional units that are being offered. Similarly, college-run diplomas may change from one academic year to another. It is the additional extras and facilities that may make a course or college more appealing for a particular programme, and prospective students should carry out comprehensive research. Employers often look for evidence of experience and it may be advantageous to choose a college that has established links with industry.

The following list includes those further education colleges offering courses for those hoping to pursue a career in catering, hotel administration and management. The list is not exhaustive and, for reasons stated above, changes frequently. It is therefore advisable to use it as a guide and request further details directly from the colleges of interest. Applications should be made to the colleges directly.

England

Accrington, Accrington & Rossendale College, Eagle Street Training Centre, Accrington, Lancashire BB5 1NS; Tel: 01254 354322; www.across.ac.uk

Altrincham, South Trafford College, Manchester Road, West Timperley, Altrincham, Cheshire WA14 5PQ; Tel: 0161 952 4600; ww.stcoll.ac.uk

Andover, Cricklade College, Charlton Road, Andover, Hampshire SP10 1EJ; Tel: 01264 363311; www.cricklade. ac.uk

Ashington, Northumberland College, College Road, Ashington NE63 9RG; Tel: 01670 841200; www.northland. ac.uk

Ashton-under-Lyne, Tameside College of Technology, Beaufort Road, Ashton-under-Lyne, Greater Manchester OL2 5TG; Tel: 0161 330 6911; www.tameside college.ac.uk

Aylesbury, Aylesbury College, Oxford Road, Aylesbury, Buckinghamshire HP21 8PD; Tel: 01296 434111

Banbury, North Oxon College, Broughton Road, Banbury, OX16 9QA; Tel: 01295 252221; www.northox.ac.uk

Barking, Barking College, Dagenham Road, Romford, Essex RM7 0XU; Tel: 01708 766841

Barnet, Barnet College,Wood Street, Barnet, Hertfordshire EN5 4AZ; Tel: 020 8440 6321; www.barnet.ac.uk

Barnsley, Barnsley College, Old Mill Lane Site, Church Street, Barnsley S70 2AX; Tel: 01226 216216

Barnstaple, North Devon College, Old Sticklepath Hill, Barnstable EX31 2BQ; Tel: 01271 388086

Barrow-in-Furness, Furness College, Howard Street, Barrow-in-Furness, Cumbria LA14 1NB; Tel: 01229 825017; www.furness.ac.uk

Basingstoke, Basingstoke College, Worting Road, Basing-stoke, Hampshire RG21 8TN; Tel: 01256 54141; www. bcot.ac.uk

Bath, City of Bath College, Avon Street, Bath BA1 1UP; Tel: 01225 312191

Bedford, Bedford College, Cauldwell Street, Bedford MK46 4HB; Tel: 01234 345151

Beverley, Beverley College, Longcroft Hall, Gallows Lane, Beverley, East Riding, Yorkshire HU17 7DT; Tel: 01482 868362

Birkenhead, Wirral Metropolitan College, Withers Lane, Wallasey L45 7LT; Tel: 0151 639 8371; www.wmc.ac.uk

Birmingham, Birmingham College of Food, Summer Row, Birmingham B3 1JB; Tel: 0121 604 1000; www.bcftcs.ac.uk

Bourneville College, Bristol Road South, Northfield, Birmingham B31 2AJ; Tel: 0121 411 1414; www.bourneville.ac.uk

East Birmingham College, Garretts Green Lane, Garretts Green, Birmingham B33 0TS; Tel: 0121 743 4471; www.ebham.ac.uk

Handsworth College, The Council House, Soho Road, Handsworth, Birmingham B26 2TB; Tel: 0121 265 1000; www.handsworth.ac.uk

Blackburn, Blackburn College, Feilden Street, Blackburn, Lancashire BB2 1LH; Tel: 01254 292143; www.blackburn.ac.uk

Blackpool, Blackpool & The Fylde College, Ashfield Road, Bispham, Blackpool FY2 0HB; Tel: 01253 352352; www.blackpool.ac.uk

Bolton, Bolton College, Manchester Road, Bolton, Greater Manchester BL2 1ER; Tel: 01204 531411

Bootle, Hugh Baird College, Balliol Road, Bootle, Merseyside L20 7EW; Tel: 0151 922 6704

Boston, Boston College, Rowley Road, Boston, Lincolnshire PE21 6JF; Tel: 01205 365701; www.boston.ac.uk

Bournemouth, Bournemouth and Poole College, The Lansdowne, Bournemouth BH1 3JJ; Tel: 01202 205831; www.bmouth-poole-cfe.ac.uk

Bradford, Bradford & Ilkley Community College, Great Horton Road, Bradford, West Yorkshire BD7 1AY; Tel: 01274 753386; www.bilk.ac.uk

Braintree, Braintree College, Church Lane, Essex CM7 5SN; Tel: 01376 321711

Bridlington, East Yorkshire College, St. Mary's Walk, Bridlington, East Riding, Yorkshire YO16 5JW; Tel: 01262 852000

Brighton, Brighton College, Pelham Street, Brighton BN1 4FA; Tel: 01273 667788; www.bricoltech.ac.uk

Bristol, Bristol College, Ashley Down, Bristol BS7 9BU; Tel: 0117 924 1241

Broadstairs, Thanet College, Ramsgate Road, Broadstairs, Kent CT10 1PN; Tel: 01843 865111

Brockenhurst, Brockenhurst College, Lyndhurst Road, Brockenhurst, Hampshire SO41 7ZW; Tel: 01590 625555; www.brock.ac.uk

Burton upon Trent, Burton College, Lichfield Street, Burton upon Trent, Staffordshire DE14 3RL; Tel: 01283 545401

Bury, Bury College, Albert Road, Whitefield, Bury, Greater Manchester M45 8NH; Tel: 0161 763 1505

Bury St Edmunds, West Suffolk College, Out Risbygate, Bury St. Edmunds, Suffolk IP33 3RL; Tel: 01298 701301; www.westsuffolk.ac.uk

Buxton, High Peak College, Harpur Hill, Buxton, Derbyshire SK17 9JZ; Tel: 01298 71100

Cambridge, Cambridge Regional College, Newmarket Road, Cambridge CB5 8EG; Tel; 01223 357743; www.camre. ac.uk

Cannock, Cannock Chase College, The Green, Cannock, Staffordshire WS11 1UE; Tel: 01543 462200

Canterbury, Canterbury College, New Dover Road, Canterbury, Kent CT1 3AJ; Tel: 01227 811111; www.cant-col.ac.uk

Carlisle, Carlisle College, Victoria Place, Carlisle, Cumbria CA1 1HS; Tel: 01228 24464

Carshalton, Carshalton College, Nightingale Road, Carshalton, Surrey SM5 2EJ; Tel: 020 8770 6800; www. carshalton.ac.uk

Chelmsford, Chelmsford College, Princes Road, Chelmsford, Essex CM2 9DX; Tel: 01245 265611; www.chelmcollege. u-net.com

Cheltenham, Gloucestershire College, 73 The Park, Cheltenham GL50 2RR; Tel: 01242 532074

Chester, West Cheshire College, Eaton Road, Handbridge, Chester CH4 7ER; Tel: 01244 677677

Chesterfield, Chesterfield College, Infirmary Road, **Chesterfield**, Derbyshire S41 7NG; Tel: 01246 500562

North Derbyshire Tertiary College, Rectory Road, Clowne, Chesterfield S43 4BQ; Tel: 01246 810 332

Chichester, Chichester College, Westgate Fields, Chichester, West Sussex PO19 1SB; Tel: 01243 786321; www.chichester.ac.uk

Chippenham, Chippenham College, Cocklebury Road, Chippenham, Wiltshire SN15 3QD; Tel: 01249 444501

Coalville, Coalville Technical College, Bridge Road, Coalville, Leicestershire LE67 3PW; Tel: 01530 836136

Colchester, Colchester Institute, Sheepen Road, Colchester, Essex CO3 3LL; Tel: 01206 718000; www.colch-inst.ac.uk

Coleford, Royal Forest of Dean College, Five Acres Campus, Coleford, Gloucestershire GL16 7JT; Tel: 01594 833416

Consett, Derwentside College, Park Road, Consett, Co Durham DH8 5EE; Tel: 01207 585900

Corby, Tresham College, George Street, Corby, Northamptonshire NN17 1QA; Tel: 01536 402252

Coventry, Henley College, Henley Road, Bell Green, Coventry CV2 1ED; Tel: 01203 611021

Crawley, Crawley College, College Road, Crawley, West Sussex RH10 1NR; Tel: 01293 612686

Crewe, South Cheshire College, Dane Bank Avenue, Crewe CW2 8AB; Tel: 01270 69133

Croydon, Croydon College, College Road, Fairfield, Croydon, Surrey CR9 1DZ; Tel: 020 8686 5700

Darlington, Darlington College, Cleveland Road, Darlington, County Durham DL3 7BB; Tel: 01325 503050

Dartford and Gravesend, North West Kent College, Miskin Road, Dartford DA1 LU; Tel: 01322 225471

Derby, Derby College, London Road, Derby DE2 8UG; Tel: 01332 757570

Dewsbury, Dewsbury College, Halifax Road, Dewsbury, West Yorkshire WF13 2AS; Tel: 01924 465916

Doncaster, Doncaster College, Waterdale Road, Doncaster, South Yorkshire DN1 3EX; Tel: 01302 553658

Durham, New College Durham, Framwellgate Moor, Durham DH1 5PB; Tel: 0191 386 2421

Eastbourne, Eastbourne College, ECAT House, Cross Levels Way, Eastbourne BN21 2HS; Tel: 01323 644711; www.ecat. ac.uk

Eastham, Wirral Metropolitan College, Carlett Park, Eastham, Wirral L62 0AY; Tel: 0151 327 4331

Eastleigh, Eastleigh College, Chestnut Avenue, Eastleigh, Hampshire SO50 6BP; Tel: 01703 326326; www. eastleigh.ac.uk

Exeter, Exeter College, Hele Road, Exeter, Devon EX4 4JS; Tel: 01392 384905

Fareham, Fareham College, Bishopsfield Road, Fareham, Hampshire PO14 1NH; Tel: 01329 815333

Farnborough, Farnborough College, Boundary Road, Farnborough, Hampshire GU14 6SB; Tel: 01252 391253

Folkestone, South Kent College, Shorncliffe Road, Folkestone CT20 2NA; Tel: 01303 850061

Grantham, Grantham College, Stonebridge Road, Grantham, Lincolnshire NG31 9AP; Tel: 01476 63141

Grays, Thurrock College, Woodview, Grays, Essex RM17 5XD; Tel: 01375 391199

Great Yarmouth, Great Yarmouth College, Southtown, Great Yarmouth, Norfolk NR31 0ED; Tel: 01493 655261

Grimsby, Grimsby College, Nuns' Corner, Grimsby, Lincolnshire DN34 5BQ; Tel: 01472 311222

Guildford, Guildford College, Stoke Park, Guildford, Surrey GU1 1EZ; Tel: 01483 448500; www.guildford.ac.uk

Halesowen, Halesowen College, Whittington Road, Halesowen, West Midlands B63 3NA; Tel: 0121 550 1451

Halifax, Calderdale College, Francis Street, Halifax, West Yorkshire HX1 3UZ; Tel: 01422 399399

Harlow, Harlow College, College Square, Harlow, Essex CM20 1LT; Tel: 01279 868000

Harrogate, Harrogate College, Hornbeam Park, Harrogate, Yorkshire HG2 8QT; Tel: 01423 879466

Harrow, Weald College, Brookshill, Harrow Weald, Middlesex HA3 6RR; Tel: 020 8420 8888

Hastings, Hastings College, Archery Road, St Leonards-on-Sea, East Sussex TN38 0HX; Tel: 01424 442222

Havant, South Downs College, College Road, Havant, Hampshire PO8 7AA; Tel: 01705 483856

Henley-on-Thames, Henley College, Deanfield Avenue, Henley-on-Thames, Oxfordshire RG9 1UH; Tel: 01494 579988; www.henley.ac.uk

Hereford, Herefordshire College, Folly Lane, Hereford HR1 1LS; Tel: 01432 352235

Hinckley, Hinckley College, London Road, Hinckley, Leicestershire LE10 1HQ; Tel: 01455 251222

Hitchin, North Hertfordshire College, Cambridge Road, Hitchin, Hertfordshire SG4 0JD; Tel: 01462 424242; www.nhc.ac.uk

Huddersfield, Huddersfield Technical College, New North Road, Huddersfield, West Yorkshire HD1 5NN; Tel: 01484 536521

Hull, Hull College, Queen's Gardens, Hull HU1 3DG; Tel: 01482 329943

Ipswich, Suffolk College, Rope Walk, Ipswich IP4 1LT; Tel: 01473 255855

Isleworth, West Thames College, London Road, Isleworth, Middlesex TW7 4HS; Tel: 020 8568 0244

Kendal, Kendal College, Minthorpe Road, Kendal, Cumbria LA9 5AY; Tel: 01539 724313

Kings Lynn, Norfolk College, Tennyson Avenue, Kings Lynn, Norfolk PE30 2QW; Tel: 01553 761144

Knowsley, Knowsley Community College, Rupert Road, Huyton, Merseyside L36 9TD; Tel: 0151 443 2658

Lancaster, Lancaster and Morecambe College, Morecambe Road, Lancaster LA1 2TY; Tel: 01524 66215

Leeds, Thomas Danby College, Roundhay Road, Sheepscar, Leeds LS7 3BG; Tel: 0113 249 4912

Leicester, Leicester South Fields College, Aylestone Road, Leicester LE2 7LW; Tel: 0116 2541818

Leigh, Wigan and Leigh College, Railway Road, Leigh, Lancashire WN7 4AH; Tel: 01942 501501

Leyland, Runshaw College, Langdale Road, Leyland, Lancashire PR5 2DQ; Tel: 01772 622677

Lincoln, North Lincolnshire College, Monks Road, Lincoln LN2 5HQ; Tel: 01522 510530

Liverpool, City of Liverpool Community College, Colquitt Street, Liverpool L1 4DB; Tel: 0151 252 1515

London, College of North West London, Priory Park Road, London NW6 7UJ; Tel: 020 8208 5000; www.cnwl.ac.uk

Hackney Community College, Chelmer Road, London E9 6BZ; Tel: 020 8533 5922; www.comm-coll-hackney.ac.uk

Hendon College, Corner Mead, Colindale, London NW9 5RA; Tel: 020 8200 8300; www.hendon.ac.uk

Lewisham College, Lewisham Way, London SE4 1UT; Tel: 020 8694 3240; www.lewisham.ac.uk

Merton College, London Road, Morden, Surrey SM4 5QX; Tel: 020 8640 3001

Newham College, High Street South, London E6 4ER; Tel: 020 8257 4000; www.newhamcfe.ac.uk

Southgate College, High Street, London N14 6BS; Tel: 020 8982 5050; www.southgate.ac.uk

Thames Valley University, St Mary's Road, London W5 5RF; Tel: 020 8231 2217; www.tvu.ac.uk

Waltham Forest College, Forest Road, London E17 4JB; Tel: 020 8501 8000; www.waltham.ac.uk

Westminster College, Vincent Square, London SW1P 2PD; Tel: 020 7828 1222

Loughborough, Loughborough College, Radmoor, Lough-borough, Leicestershire LE11 3BT; Tel: 01509 583521

Lowestoft, Lowestoft College, St Peter's Street, Lowestoft, Suffolk NR32 2NB; Tel: 01502 583521; www.lowestoft.ac.uk

Luton, Barnfield College, New Bedford Road, Luton, Bedfordshire LU2 7BF; Tel: 01582 569644; www.barnfield. demon.co.uk

Macclesfield, Macclesfield College, Park Lane, Macclesfield, Cheshire SK11 8LF; Tel: 01625 427744

Maidstone, Mid Kent College, Oakwood Park, Tonbridge Road, Maidstone ME16 8AQ; Tel: 01622 691555

Manchester, City College, Fielden Centre, 141 Barlow Moor Road, West Didsbury, Manchester M20 2PQ; Tel: 0161 957 1664

Manchester College, Lower Hardman Street, Manchester M3 3ER; Tel:0161 953 5995

Mansfield, West Nottinghamshire College, Derby Road, Mansfield NG18 5BH; Tel: 01623 27191

Melton Mowbray, Melton Mowbray College, Asfordby Road, Melton Mowbray, Leicestershire LE13 0HJ; Tel: 01664 67431

Middlesbrough, Middlesbrough College, Roman Road, Linthorpe, Middlesbrough, Cleveland TS5 5PJ; Tel: 01642 333333

Milton Keynes, Milton Keynes College, Bletchley Centre, Sherwood Drive, Bletchley, Milton Keynes MK3 6DR; Tel: 01908 68411

Nelson, Nelson and Colne College, Scotland Road, Nelson, Lancashire BB9 7YT; Tel: 01282 440332

Newbury, Newbury College, Oxford Road, Newbury, Berkshire RG13 1PQ; Tel: 01635 37000

Newcastle upon Tyne, Newcastle College, Sandyford Road, Newcastle upon Tyne NE1 8QE; Tel: 0191 200 4600

Newport, Isle of Wight College, Medina Way, Newport PO30 5TA; Tel: 01983 526631

Northampton, Northampton College, Booth Lane, Northampton NN3 3RF; Tel: 01604 734567

Northwich, Mid Cheshire College, Northwich CW8 1LJ; Tel: 01606 74444

Norwich, Norwich Hotel School, City College, Ipswich Road, Norwich NR15 1JY; Tel: 01603 773391

Nottingham, Clarendon College, Pelham Avenue, Nottingham NG5 1AL; Tel: 0115 953 4205

Nuneaton, North Warwickshire and Hinckley College, Hinckley Road, Nuneaton CV11 6BH; Tel: 01203 349321

Oldham, Oldham College, Rochdale Road, Oldham, Lancashire OL9 6AA; Tel: 0161 624 5214

Oxford, Oxford College of Further Education, Oxpens Road, Oxford OX1 1SA; Tel: 01865 245871

Peterborough, Peterborough Regional College, Park Crescent, Peterborough, Cambridgeshire PE1 1DZ; Tel: 01733 67366

Peterlee, East Durham Community College, Howletch Site, Peterlee, County Durham SR8 1NU; Tel: 0191 518 2000

Plymouth, College of Further Education, Devonport, Plymouth, Devon PL1 5QG; Tel: 01752 385186

Portsmouth, Highbury College, Dovercourt Road, Cosham, Portsmouth PO6 2SA; Tel: 01705 283261

Preston, Preston College, St. Vincent's Road, Fulwood, Preston PR2 4UR; Tel: 01772 772200

Reading, Reading College, Crescent Road, Reading, Berkshire RG1 5RQ; Tel: 01734 583501

Redbridge, Redbridge College, Little Heath, Romford, Essex RM6 4XT; Tel: 020 8599 5231

Redditch, North East Worcestershire College, Peakman Street, Redditch B98 8DW; Tel: 01527 572525

Redhill, East Surrey College, Gatton Point South, College Crescent, Redhill RH1 2FA; Tel: 01737 772611

Redruth, Cornwall College, Pool, Redruth TR15 3RD; Tel: 01209 712 911; www.physcorn.demon.co.uk

Rochdale, Hopwood Hall College, St. Mary's Gate, Rochdale OL12 6RY; Tel: 01706 345346

Romford, Havering College, Tring Gardens, Harold Hill, Romford, Essex RM3 9ES; Tel: 01708 462840

Rotherham, Rotherham College, Eastwood Lane, Rotherham, South Yorkshire S65 1EG; Tel: 01709 362111

Rugby, Rugby College, Lower Hillmorton Road, Rugby, Warwickshire CV21 3QS; Tel: 01788 541666

St Austell, St Austell College, Trevarthian Road, St Austell, Cornwall PL25 4BW; Tel: 01726 67911

St Helens, St Helens College, Brook Street, St Helens, Merseyside WA10 1PZ; Tel: 01744 733766

Salford, University of Salford, Allerton Building, Frederick Road, Salford M6 6PU; 0161 736 6541

Salisbury, Salisbury College, Southampton Road, Salisbury, Wiltshire SP1 2LW; Tel: 01722 323711

Scarborough, Yorkshire Coast College, Lady Edith's Drive, Scarborough YO12 5RN; Tel: 01723 372105

Scunthorpe, North Lindsey College, Kingsway, Scunthorpe, North Lincolnshire DN17 1AJ; Tel: 01724 294070

Selby, Selby College, Abbot's Road, Selby, North Yorkshire YO8 8AT; Tel: 01757 211000

Sheffield, Sheffield College, Castle Centre, Granville Road, Sheffield S2 2RL; Tel: 0114 260 2100

Shrewsbury, Radbrook College, Radbrook Road, Shrewbury SY3 9BL; Tel: 01743 232686

Skipton, Craven Cottage, High Street, Skipton, North Yorkshire BD23 1JY; Tel: 01756 791411

Slough, Thames Valley University, Wellington Street, Slough SL1 1YG; Tel: 01753 697601

Solihull, Solihull College, Blossomfield Road, Solihull, West Midlands B91 1SB; Tel: 0121 711 2111

Southampton, Southampton City College, St Mary Street, Southampton SO14 1AR; Tel: 01703 635222

Southend-on-Sea, South East Essex College, Carnarvon Road, Southend-on-Sea, Essex SS2 6LS; Tel: 01702 220400

Southport, Southport College, Mornington Road, Southport, Merseyside PR9 0TT; Tel: 01704 500606

South Shields, South Tyneside College, St George's Avenue, South Shields NE34 6ET; Tel: 0191 427 3500

Stafford, Stafford College, Earl Street, Stafford ST16 2QR; Tel: 01785 223800

Stamford, Stamford College, Drift Road, Stamford, Lincolnshire PE9 1XA; Tel: 01780 64141

Stockport, North Area College, Buckingham Road, Heaton Moor, Stockport, Cheshire SK4 4RA; Tel: 0161 442 7494

Stoke-on-Trent, Stoke-on-Trent College, Stoke Road, Shelton, Stoke-on-Trent, ST4 2DG; Tel: 01782 208208

Stratford-upon-Avon, Stratford-upon-Avon College, The Willows North, Alcester Road, Stratford-upon-Avon, Warwickshire CV37 9QR; Tel: 01789 266245

Street, Strode College, Church Road, Street, Somerset BA16 0AB; Tel: 01458 844400

Sunderland, City of Sunderland College, Swan Street, Sunderland SR5 1EB; Tel: 0191 516 2000

Swindon, Swindon College, North Star Avenue, Swindon SN2 1DY; Tel: 01793 498300

Tamworth, Tamworth College, Croft Street, Upper Gungate, Tamworth, Staffordshire B79 8AE; Tel: 01827 310202

Taunton, Somerset College, Wellington Road, Taunton TA1 5AX; Tel: 01823 366366

Telford, Telford College, Haybridge Road, Wellington, Telford, Shropshire TF2 2NP; Tel: 01952 642200

Tiverton, East Devon College, Bolham Road, Tiverton EX16 6SH; Tel: 01884 235200

Tonbridge, West Kent College, Brook Street, Tonbridge TN9 2PW; Tel: 01732 358101

Torquay, South Devon College, Newton Road, Torquay TQ2 5BY; Tel: 01803 386338

Trowbridge, Trowbridge College, College Road, Trowbridge, Wiltshire BA14 0ES; Tel: 01225 766241

Twickenham, Richmond upon Thames College, Egerton Road, Twickenham, Middlesex TW2 7SJ; Tel: 020 8607 8000

Uxbridge, Uxbridge College, Park Road, Uxbridge, Middlesex UB8 1NQ; Tel: 01895 230411

Wakefield, Wakefield College, Margaret Street, Wakefield, West Yorkshire WF1 2DH; Tel: 01924 789393

Wallsend, North Tyneside College, Embleton Avenue, Wallsend NE26 1AG; Tel: 0191 229 5302

Walsall, Walsall College, St Paul's Street, Walsall, West Midlands WS1 1XN; Tel: 01922 657000

Ware, Hertford Regional College, Scotts Road, Ware, Hertfordshire SG12 9JF; Tel: 01920 465441; www.hertreg.ac.uk

Watford, West Herts College, Cassio Campus, Langley Road, Watford WD1 3RH; Tel: 01923 812565; www.westherts. ac.uk

Wath upon Dearne, Dearne Valley College, West Street, Wath upon Dearne, Rotherham, South Yorkshire S63 6PX; Tel: 01709 760310

West Bromwich, Sandwell College, High Street, West Bromwich, West Midlands B70 8DU; Tel: 0121 254 6612

Weston-Super-Mare, Weston College, Knightstone Road, Weston-Super-Mare BS23 2AL; Tel: 01934 411411

Weybridge, Brooklands College, Heath Road, Weybridge, Surrey KT13 8TT; Tel: 01932 853300

Weymouth, Weymouth College, Newstead Road, Weymouth, Dorset DT4 0DX; Tel: 01305 208967

Widnes, Halton College, Kingsway, Widnes, Cheshire, WA8 7QQ; Tel: 0151 423 1391

Wigan, Wigan and Leigh College, Parson's Walk, Wigan, Lancashire WN1 1RS; Tel: 01942 501501

Wolverhampton, Bilston Community College, Westfield Road, Bilston, Wolverhampton WV14 6ER; Tel: 01902 821037

Worcester, Worcester College, Deansway, Worcester WR1 2JF; Tel: 01905 723383

Workington, West Cumbria College, Park Lane, Workington CA14 2RW; Tel: 01900 64331

Worksop, North Nottinghamshire College, Carlton Road, Worksop S81 7HP; Tel: 01909 473561

Worthing, Northbrook College, Littlehampton Road, Goring-by-Sea, Worthing BN12 6NU; Tel: 01903 830057

Yeovil, Yeovil College, Mudford Road, Yeovil, Somerset BA21 4DR; Tel: 01935 23921

York, York College, Tadcaster Road, York, YO2 1UA; Tel: 01904 770200

Careers in Catering, Hotel Administration and Management

Channel Islands

Guernsey, Guernsey College, Route des Coutanchez, St Peter Port, Guernsey GY1 2TT; Tel: 01481 727121

Jersey, Highlands College, St Saviour, Jersey JE4 9QA; Tel: 01534 608608
Cambridge Tutorial College, College House, Leoville, St Ouen, Jersey JE3 2DB; 01534 485052

Northern Ireland

Antrim, North East Institute, Fountain Street, Antrim BT41 4AL; Tel: 01849 463916
Armagh, Armagh College, Lonsdale Street, Armagh BT61 7HN; Tel: 01861 522205

Ballymena, North East Institute, Trostan Avenue, Ballymena, Co Antrim BT43 7BN; Tel: 01266 652871
Ballymoney, Causeway Institute, 2 Coleraine Road, Ballymoney, Co Antrim BT51 6BP; Tel: 012656 62258
Banbridge, Upper Bann Institute, Castlewellan Road, Banbridge BT32 4AY; Tel: 018206 62289; www.ubifhe.ac.uk
Bangor, North Down and Ards Institute, Castle Park Road, Bangor BT20 4TF; Tel: 01247 271254
Belfast, Belfast Institute, Brunswick Street, Belfast BT2 7GX; Tel: 01232 265165
Castlereagh College, Montgomery Road, Belfast BT6 9JD; Tel: 01232 797144

Coleraine, Causeway Institute, Union Street, Coleraine, County Derry BT52 1QA; Tel: 01265 662258

Downpatrick, East Down Institute, Market Street, Downpatrick BT30 6ND; Tel: 01396 615815
Dungannon, East Tyrone College, Circular Road, Dungannon BT71 6BQ; Tel: 01868 722323

Enniskillen, Fermanagh College, Fairview, 1 Dublin Road, Enniskillen BT22 6AE; Tel: 01365 322431

Larne, East Antrim Institute, 32–34 Pond Street, Larne BT40 1SQ; Tel: 01232 864331

Limavady, Limavady College, Main Street, Limavady BT49 0EX; Tel: 015047 62334

Lisburn, Lisburn College, 39 Castle Street, Lisburn BT27 4SU; Tel: 01846 677225

Londonderry, North West Institute, Strand Road, Londonderry BT487BY; Tel: 01504 266711

Lurgan, Upper Bann Institute, 26-44 Lurgan Road, Portadown, Craigavon BT63 5BL; Tel: 01762 337111

Magherafelt, North East Institute, 22 Moneymore Road, Magherafelt, Co Londonderry BT45 6AE; Tel: 01648 32462

Newcastle, East Down Institute, 2 Donard Street, Newcastle BT33 0AP; Tel: 013967 22451

Newry, Newry College, Patrick Street, Newry BT35 8DN; Tel: 01693 61071

Newton Abbey, East Antrim Institute, 400 Shore Road, Newton Abbey BT37 9RS; Tel: 01232 855000

Newtownards, North Down and Ards Institute, Victoria Avenue, Newtownards BT23 7ED; Tel: 01247 812116

Omagh, Omagh College, Mountjoy Road, Omagh, Co Tyrone BT79 7AH; Tel: 01662 245433

Portadown, Upper Bann Institute, 26-44 Lurgan Road, Portadown BT63 5BL; Tel: 01762 337111

Portrush, Northern Ireland Hotel and Catering College, Ballywillan Road, Portrush, County Antrim BT56 8JL; Tel: 01265 823768

Wales

Aberdare, Aberdare College, Cwmdare Road, Aberdare CF44 8ST; Tel: 01685 887500; www.aberdare.ac.uk

Aberystwyth, Coleg Ceredigion, Llanbadard Fawr, Aberystwyth SY23 3BP; Tel: 01970 624511; www.ceredigion.ac.uk

Bangor, Coleg Menai, Ffriddoedd Road, Bangor LL57 2TP; Tel: 01248 370125; www.menai.ac.uk

Barry, Barry College, Colcot Road, Barry CF6 8YJ; Tel: 01446 743519; www.barry.academic.uk

Brecon, Coleg Powys Brecon, Penlan, Brecon LD3 9SR; Tel: 01874 625252; www.coleg powys.ac.uk

Bridgend, Bridgend College, Cowbridge Road, Bridgend; CF31 3DF; Tel: 01656 679337; www.bridgend.ac.uk

Cardiff, University of Wales, Colchester Avenue, Cardiff CF3 7XR; Tel: 01222 506300; www.uwic.ac.uk

Cardigan, Coleg Ceredigion, Park Place, Cardigan SA43 1AB; Tel: 01239 612032; www.ceredigion.ac.uk

Carmarthen, Carmarthenshire College, Carmarthen SA31 2NH; Tel: 01554 748000 www.ccta.ac.uk

Colwyn Bay, Llandrillo College, Llandudno Road, Rhos-on-Sea, Colwyn Bay LL28 4HZ; Tel: 01492 546666; www.llandrillo.ac.uk

Connah's Quay, Deeside College, Kelsterton Road, Connah's Quay, Deeside CH5 4BR; Tel: 01244 831531

Crosskeys, Gwent College, Risca Road, Crosskeys NP1 7FR; Tel: 01495 333456; www.gwent-tertiary.ac.uk

Dolgellau, Coleg Meirion-Dwyfor, Ffordd Ty'n y Coed, Dolgellau, Gwynedd LL40 2SW; Tel: 01341 422827; www.meiron.dwyfor.ac.uk

Ebbw Vale, Gwent Tertiary College, College Road, Ebbw Vale NP3 6LE; Tel: 01495 333000; www.gwent-tertiary.ac.uk

Haverfordwest, Pembrokeshire College, Merlins Bridge, Haverfordwest SA61 1SZ; Tel: 01437 765247; www.pembrokeshire.ac.uk

Merthyr Tydfil, Merthyr Tydfil College, Ynysfach Road, Ynysfach, Merthyr Tydfil CF48 1AR; Tel: 01685 726000; www.merthyr.ac.uk

Neath, Neath College, Dwr-y-Felin Road, Neath SA10 7RF; Tel: 01639 634271; www.neath.ac.uk

Newport, Gwent Tertiary College, Nash Road, Newport NP9 0TS; Tel: 01633 466000

Newtown, Coleg Powys, Llanidloes Road, Newtown SY16 6HU; Tel: 01686 622722; www.coleg-powys.ac.uk

Pontypool, Gwent Tertiary College, Blaendare Road, Pontypool NP4 5YE; Tel: 01495 762242

Pontypridd, Coleg Pontypridd, Ynys Terrace, Rhydyfelin, Pontypridd CF35 6EL; Tel: 01443 662280; www.ponty-pridd.ac.uk

Swansea, Swansea College, Tycoch Road, Sketty, Swansea SA2 9EB; Tel: 01792 284100; www.swannncoll.ac.uk

Tonypandy, Rhondda College, Llwynpia, Tonypandy CF40 2TQ; Tel: 01443 662800

Ystrad Mynach, Ystrad Mynach College, Twyn Road, Ystrad Mynach, Hengoed CF81 7XR; Tel: 01443 816888, www.ystrad-mynach.ac.uk

Scotland

Aberdeen, Aberdeen College, Gallowgate, Aberdeen AB9 1DN; Tel: 01224 612000; www.abcol.ac.uk

Alloa, Clackmannan College, Branshill Road, Alloa FK10 3BT; Tel: 01259 215121; www.medc.paisley.ac.uk

Arbroath, Angus College, Keptie Road, Arbroath DD11 3EA; Tel: 01241 432600; www angus.ac.uk

Ayr, Ayr College, Dam Park, Ayr KA8 0EU; Tel: 01292 613231; www.ayrcoll.ac.uk

Bathgate, West Lothian College, Marjoribanks Street, Bathgate EH48 1QJ; Tel: 01506 634300; www.west-lothian.co.uk

Clydebank, Clydebank College, Kilbowie Road, Clydebank G81 2AA; Tel: 0141 952 7771; www.clydebank.ac.uk

Cumbernauld, Cumbernauld College, Tryst Road, Town Centre, Cumbernauld G67 1HU; Tel: 01236 731811

Cupar, Elmwood College, Carslogie Road, Cupar KY15 4JB; Tel: 01334 658800

Dalkeith, Jewel and Esk Valley College, Eskbank Centre, Newbattle Road, Dalkeith EH22 3AE; Tel: 0131 660 1010; www.jevc.ac.uk

Dumfries, Dumfries and Galloway College, Heathhall, Dumfries DG1 3QZ; Tel: 01387 261261

Dundee, Dundee College, Old Glamis Road, Dundee DD3 8LE; 01382 834834; www.dundeecoll.ac.uk

Dunfermline, Lauder College, Halbeath Road, Dunfermline KY11 5DY; Tel: 01383 845000; www.lauder.ac.uk

East Kilbride, Cambuslang College, 86–88 Main Street, East Kilbride G74 4JY; Tel: 013552 270750; www.rmplc.co.uk

Edinburgh, Edinburgh Technical College, Crewe Toll, Edinburgh EH4 2NZ; Tel: 0131 332 2491; www.ed-coll.ac.uk

Elgin, Moray College, Moray Street, Elgin IV30 1NX; Tel: 01343 554321; www.moray.ac.uk

Falkirk, Falkirk College, Grangemouth Road, Falkirk FK2 9AD; Tel: 01324 403000; www.falkirkcollege.ac.uk

Fraserburgh, Banff and Buchan College, Henderson Road, Fraserburgh AB43 5GA; Tel: 01346 515777

Glasgow, Glasgow College, 230 Cathedral Street, Glasgow G1 2TG; Tel: 0141 552 3751

John Wheatley College, 1345 Shettleston Road, Glasgow G32 9AT; Tel: 0141 778 2426; www.jwheatley.ac.uk

Glenrothes, Glenrothes College, Stenton Road, Glenrothes KY6 2RA; Tel: 01592 775268

Greenock, James Watt College, Finnart Street, Greenock PA16 8HF; Tel: 01475 553047; www.jameswatt.co.uk

Hawick, Borders College, Henderson Building, Commercial Road, Hawick TD9 7AW; Tel: 01450 374191

Inverness, Inverness College, 3 Longman Road, Longman South, Inverness IV1 1SA; Tel: 01463 236681

Irvine, Kilmarnock College, Bank Street Campus, Irvine KA12 0LP; Tel: 01294 311259; www.kilmarnock.ac.uk

Kirkcaldy, Fife College, St Brycedale Avenue, Kirkcaldy KY1 1EX; Tel: 01592 268591; www.fife.ac.uk

Kirkwall, Orkney College, Kirkwall, Orkney KW15 1QN; Tel: 01856 872839

Lerwick, Shetland College, Gremista, Lerwick ZE1 0PX; Tel: 01595 695514; www.tcuhi.ac.uk

Motherwell, Motherwell College, Dalzell Drive, Motherwell ML1 2DD; Tel: 01698 232323

Paisley, Reid Kerr College, Renfrew Road, Paisley PA3 4DR; Tel: 0141 889 4225

Perth, Perth College, Crieff Road, Perth PH1 2NX; Tel: 01738 621171; www.uni.ac.uk

Stornoway, Lewis Castle College, Stornoway, Isle of Lewis HS2 0HR; Tel: 01851 707019

Thurso, Thurso College, Ormlie Road, Thurso KW14 7EE; Tel: 01847 896161; www.uni.ac.uk

Degree and postgraduate courses

Degree and Higher National Diploma programmes are offered by colleges and universities to those who have already successfully completed a GNVQ Advanced, BTEC National Diploma, A levels, or an equivalent programme that the university deems acceptable. Students completing a course at this level will have the opportunity of seeking employment at supervisory level, trainee or junior management. Degree courses are popular, due to the high demand for qualified personnel at management level. Courses may change annually and new courses are developed. Applications are normally made through UCAS, the Universities and Colleges Admissions Service, and exact entry requirements may vary. For example, a prerequisite for a one-year BA degree will almost certainly be an approved HND in a related subject. Some colleges offer HND programmes as a franchise from a university, allowing high-calibre students to transfer after their initial course.

Masters degrees are usually undertaken by those who have both industrial experience at managerial level and a first degree.

For further information on higher-level courses contact UCAS, the Universities and Colleges Admission Service, PO Box 67, Cheltenham, Gloucestershire GL50 3SF; Tel: 01242 222444.

12 Other forms of training

In-house training

Many hotel and catering companies offer in-house training. This means that you will be given training while you are employed, and will be paid. The training may involve working in various departments of an hotel or at a number of restaurant outlets within a group. Some employers may send you on part-time college courses, in order to gain professional and specialist qualifications. Training may be for craft or trainee management positions, and starting qualifications range from a school record of achievements through to degree level. The period of training may vary from several months to three years, depending on the individual programme. Each provides a wide variety of changing opportunities and so it is best to contact the employer directly. This list is not conclusive but provides opportunity for investigation.

Allied Domecq Inns, 107 Station Street, Burton on Trent, Staffordshire DE14 1BZ; Tel: 01283 545320
Allied Leisure plc, Commercial Centre, Tower Park, Poole, Dorset DH12 4NY; Tel: 01202 716010
Aramark plc (managed services), Aramark House, 69 Honey End Lane, Tilehurst, Reading RG30 4QL; Tel: 0118 959 6761

Bass Leisure Ltd, New Castle House, Castle Boulevard, Nottingham NG7 1FT; Tel: 0115 948 4333; www.bass.com

Beefeater (restaurants and pubs), Building 3, The Herculean, Houghton Hall Office Park, Porz Avenue, Dunstable, Bedfordshire LU5 5XE; Tel: 01582 844295

Bourne Leisure Group Ltd, Normandy Court, 1 Wolsey Road, Hemel Hempstead, Hertfordshire HP2 4TU; Tel: 01442 241658

Conran Restaurants, The Clove Building, Magure Street, London SE1 2NQ; Tel: 020 7716 0716

Debenhams Food Services, Debenhams MTP, 1 Welbeck Street, London W1A 1DE

Glendola Leisure Ltd, 86 East Lane, Wembley, Middlesex HA0 3NJ; Tel: 020 8904 8277

Granada Hospitality, PO Box 218, Toddington, Bedfordshire LU5 6QG; Tel: 01525 878341

Group Chez Gerard Ltd, 8 Upper Street, St Martin's Lane, London WC2H 9EN; Tel: 020 7240 9240

Harrods Ltd, 87–135 Brompton Road, Knightsbridge, London SW1X 7XL; Tel: 020 7730 1234

The Hatton Hotel Group, Hatton Court, Upton Hill, Gloucester GL4 8DE; Tel: 01452 617412

Jarvis Hotels Ltd, Wye House, London Road, High Wycombe, Buckinghamshire HP11 1LH; Tel: 01494 428806

McDonald's Restaurants Ltd, 11–59 High Road, East Finchley, London N2 8AW; Tel: 020 8883 6400

Marston Hotels, The Mews, Prince's Parade, Hythe, Kent CT21 6AQ; Tel: 01303 269900

The Pelican Group plc, 78 Wardour Street, London W1V 4PL; Tel: 020 7478 8085

Quadrant Catering (contract catering), Dorcan House, Elding Drive, Swindon SN3 3UY; Tel: 01793 546500

Scottish and Newcastle Retail (pub and restaurants division), Riverside House, Riverside Way, Northampton NN1 5NU; Tel: 01604 239000

Stakis plc (hotel and catering), 3 Atlantic Quay, York Streeet, Glasgow G2 8JH; Tel: 0141 204 4321

Swallow Hotels Ltd, PO Box 30, Swallow House, Parsons Road, Washington, Tyne and Wear NE37 1QS; Tel: 0191 419 4545

Thistle Hotels, 2 The Calls, Leeds LS2 7JU; Tel: 01132439111

Travel Inn, Oakley House, Oakley Road, Leagrove Luton LU4 9QH; Tel: 01582 499297

Whitbread Inns, Park Square Chambers, 14 Park Street, Luton, Bedfordshire LU1 3EP; Tel: 01582 455666

Whitbread plc, Whitbread House, Park Street West, Luton LU1 3BG; Tel: 0870 242 2020; www.whitbread.com

Private cookery schools

This section provides details of a number of the major private cookery schools in the UK for tuition leading to diplomas and certificates. Due to industry-led demand, the type, content and fees of these courses change periodically and should be checked for accuracy with the school. Some private schools have accommodation available. Those listed are for guidance only. Specialist food magazines, available from newsagents, may also provide advertisements for additional schools and courses that may be established.

The Bath School of Cookery

Basset House, Claverton, Bath, Avon BA2 7BL; Tel: 01225 722498

First opened in 1988. Students can enrol on a wide range of courses and take advantage of a herb, vegetable and fruit garden.

Bonne Bouche

Lower Beers, Brithem Bottom, Devon, EX15 1NB

Provides residential courses in a listed 16th-century Devon longhouse. Classes have a maximum of six students.

Le Cordon Bleu (London)

114 Marylebone Lane, London W1M 6HH; Tel: 020 7935 3503

Cordon Bleu, meaning blue ribbon, has been synonymous with culinary excellence since the 16th century. Now famous worldwide, the London school was founded in 1933 by Rosemary Hume, a Paris Cordon Bleu graduate. Students have included royalty and many leading personalities in the world of cookery including writers, teachers, journalists and restaurateurs. The culinary art of Le Cordon Bleu is reflected in a long history of publishing. Le Cordon Bleu bistros, cafes, tea rooms and boutiques can be found around the world.

Cordon Vert

The Vegetarian Society, Parkdale, Dunham Road, Altrincham, Cheshire WA14 4QG; Tel: 0161 928 0793

The Cordon Vert Cookery School is unique in that it is part of the Vegetarian Society, the recognized authority on vegetarian food and related issues. There are over 4 million strict vegetarians and a further 10 million actively reducing their meat intake in the United Kingdom. The school offers valuable education and training in food preparation for vegetarians far removed from traditional thoughts of omelettes, progressing towards ingredients including carob syrup, Quorn and tamari. Courses can be either residential or non-residential.

La Cuisine Imaginaire, the Vegetarian Cookery School

18 Belmont Court, Belmont Hill, St Albans, Herts AL1 1RB;
Tel: 01727 837643

Short courses are offered on subjects to include dinner party
cookery, seasonal suppers, dine and wine, dairy and gluten free,
Christmas cuisine, and vegetarian cuisine around the world.

Edinburgh Cookery School

The Coach House, Newliston, Kirkliston, Edinburgh EH29
9EB; Tel: 0131 667 3960

The cookery school is in a former 18th-century coach house
on Newliston country estate. It provides a friendly 'farmhouse'
atmosphere with practical hands-on experience to achieve
professional standards. There is limited accommodation. On
completion of many courses, students are employed in ski
chalets, yachts and shooting lodges throughout the world.

The Grange

Whatley, Frome, Somerset BA11 3LA; 01373 836579

Cookery at The Grange was founded in 1981 to provide intensive courses for career cooks. Set in a specifically converted
17th-century coach house, it has its own fruit, vegetable and
herb gardens. Each course has a maximum intake of 16 and
provides tuition on cuisine from afar. Course fees include
accommodation and meals. Past students are now employed
around the world on yachts, in ski resorts and other exciting
places.

Harrow House

1 Silverdale Road, Eastbourne, East Sussex BN20 7AA; Tel:
01323 730851

Formerly Eastbourne College of Food and Fashion, this school has recently been refurbished. All courses lead to a National Vocational Qualification.

Leith's School of Food and Wine

21 St Alban's Grove, London W8 5BP; Tel: 020 7229 0177

Established in 1975, the school provides professional training for career cooks and short courses and demonstrations for amateurs. Courses are non-residential.

The Manor School of Fine Cuisine

Old Melton Road, Widmerpool, Nottinghamshire NG12 5QL; Tel: 01949 81371

The Manor is a residential cookery school, formerly a staging post, built in the 17th century. It provides for a range of qualifications; courses vary from one evening to four weeks.

Tante Marie School of Cookery

Woodham House, Carlton Road, Woking, Surrey GU21 4HF; Tel: 01483 726957

Founded in 1954, this has an international reputation. It is a day school, although help may be given in finding accommodation. All courses at present attract a 24 per cent vocational training tax relief, a procedure dealt with by the college. Uniform, books and knives are chargeable extras.

Courses in hotel and restaurant management

Schiller International School of Tourism and Hospitality Management

Royal Waterloo House, 51–55 Waterloo Road, London SE1 8TX; Tel: 020 7928 8484

Schiller International is an independent American university, offering a wide range of first and postgraduate degrees in international hotel and tourism management. There are ten campuses in six countries. The associate and bachelor degrees have been accredited by the Hotel, Catering and International Management Association, and place an emphasis on combining basic business studies with practical hotel and restaurant management training.

13 Useful addresses and information

British Hospitality Association

Queen's House, 55–56 Lincoln's Inn Fields, London WC2A 3BH; Tel: 020 7404 7744

The British Hospitality Association has been representing the hotel, restaurant and catering industry for over 90 years. It is the UK's national association and represents over 20,000 establishments, ensuring that the views of the industry are made clear to the government. The current manifesto reviews policies for licensing laws, taxation, employment and training, marketing, European issues, motorway service areas and deregulation. As a major force, it intends to influence the government with regard to the rate of value added tax within the industry, highlighting the major opportunities a lower rate would bring, including the creation of new jobs and the generation of additional income. It also acknowledges the need to provide good-quality training through NVQs and Modern Apprenticeships. It has a national council and nine divisional committees elected by members in the counties. A major objective of the committees is to raise the profile of the industry and to encourage more bright young people to join it by promoting the highest standards of conduct and by 'talking up' the industry to consumers, investors, schools and parents.

British Institute of Innkeeping

Park House, 24 Park Street, Camberley, Surrey GU15 3PL; Tel: 01276 684449; www.barzone.co.uk

The British Institute of Innkeeping is currently the most popular individual membership organization in the licensed retail trade. New qualifications were launched in 1996, equivalent to NVQs levels 3 and 4, aimed at providing a national standard in a range of popular subject areas. The certificates, aimed at publicans and senior public house staff, are in the areas of:

◆ catering management;
◆ financial management;
◆ business development.

Business and Technology Education Council/Edexcel

Stewart House, 32 Russell Square, London WC1B 5DN; Tel: 020 7393 4444; www.edexcel.org.uk

The Business and Technology Education Council (BTEC) is an awarding and assessment body for NVQs and GNVQs accredited by NCVQ in the hospitality and catering industry. Within the industry it is historically recognized for its BTEC First, National and Higher National Diplomas, which lead towards supervisory and management positions. Most of these are full-time courses, although BTEC has certificates that are for part-time students. The First and National programmes in hotel and catering are currently being replaced by the GNVQ Intermediate and Advanced courses in hospitality and catering, also awarded by BTEC.

Caterer and Hotelkeeper

Quadrant House, The Quadrant, Sutton, Surrey SM2 5AS; Tel: 020 8652 8680

This weekly publication provides articles and information on a wide range of issues affecting the industry. Features may include, for example, new hygiene legislation, tips from chefs, readers' letters, new styles of restaurants or hotels. A popular feature is the appointments section, full of advertisements and opportunities, from chefs to managers, receptionists and house-keepers. Each year it publishes a careers guide for those tempted to join the industry. The magazine is available from newsagents and is published by the Reed Publishing Group.

City and Guilds of London Institute

1 Giltspur Street, London EC1A 9DD; Tel: 020 7294 2468; www.city-and-guilds.co.uk

Founded in 1878, City and Guilds is the largest assessment and awarding body of qualifications in the hotel, catering and hospitality industry within the UK. It has a wide range of NVQs accredited by NCVQ at all levels.

European Catering Association (Great Britain)

Bourne House, Horsell Park, Woking, Surrey GU21 4LY; Tel: 01483 765111

The Association acts as a spokesperson for those involved in welfare catering as the largest employer of the catering industry. Its aims include being a source of up-to-date information on catering trends, legislation and new products. Additionally, it assists with education and training in the business and welfare sector of the industry.

Hospitality Training Foundation

3rd Floor, International House, 7 High Street, London W5 5DB; Tel: 020 8579 2400; www.htf.org.uk

The Hotel and Catering Training Company became the Hospitality Training Foundation on 1 May 1996, in order to more accurately reflect and separate the activities previously conducted under one title. The Foundation's main role is to improve information about training throughout the industry and work towards developing qualifications. These activities are financially supported by the three trading divisions: The Stonebow Group, The Hospitality Awarding Body and the Hotel and Catering Training Company. As a commercial venture, they provide training and support materials for the hotel and catering industry. The Stonebow Group concentrates on offering short courses, training and consultancy services to companies intending to introduce training. The Hospitality Awarding Body awards NVQs and SVQs to trainees. The Hotel and Catering Training Company provides youth and adult training programmes and Modern Apprenticeships.

For further information, apply to the Hospitality Training Foundation.

Hotel and Catering International Management Association

191 Trinity Road, London SW17 7HN; Tel: 020 8672 4251; www.hcima.org.uk

Established in 1971, the HCIMA is the professional body for managers and potential managers in the international hospitality industry. The objectives of the Association include:

♦ the promotion of standards of good practice in catering and accommodation management;
♦ the advancement of education and training and the promotion of research.

Membership is available at five levels: Fellow, Member, Associate, Intermediate and Student. The first three categories entitle the member to use designatory letters, FHCIMA, MHCIMA and AHCIMA respectively. Membership benefits include the management magazine *Hospitality*, the use of the library and information services, careers advice and various offers, discounts and promotions.

Housekeepers' Association

Flat 7, 14–15 Molyneux Street, London W1H 5HU; Tel: 020 7724 7378

The UK Housekeepers' Association was formed in May 1985 with the support of the *Caterer and Hotelkeeper* and with Lord Forte as its patron. It has over 1,000 professional members throughout the UK involved in all aspects of housekeeping management including hotels, institutions and hospitals. There are three main objectives:

◆ improve the professional status of housekeepers;
◆ promote housekeeping as a career;
◆ provide a forum for the exchange of information and ideas.

There is an annual conference and dinner dance where house-keepers, general managers and associates meet. Invitations also include speakers and sponsors. Throughout the year, informal meetings are held, where members are invited to discuss house-keeping issues. A guest speaker is usually invited who may speak seriously on legal issues, for example, or may be light-hearted and entertaining, for example, an actor who regularly stays in hotels and can provide anecdotes. There are several regions to the Association throughout the UK and all house-keepers and students on housekeeping courses are invited to seek membership.

Institute of Food Science and Technology

5 Cambridge Court, 210 Shepherd's Bush Road, London W6 7NJ; Tel: 020 7603 6316

Certain college courses such as an HND in Science, Technology and Food give direct entry to membership of the Institute.

Institute of Home Economics

21 Portland Place; London W1N3AF; Tel: 020 7436 5677

The Institute is the national professional body for home economists. Graduates in home economics are entitled to corporate membership, together with those who hold other recognized and related qualifications. The Institute has been involved with the examining bodies, including City and Guilds and BTEC, for the development of courses at all levels. Home economists are employed in business and industry, as journalists, for recipe development and in cookery photography.

The Royal Institute of Public Health and Hygiene

28 Portland Place, London W1N 4DE; Tel: 020 7580 2731; www.riphh.org.uk

The Royal Institute, formed in 1937, sets controls and moderates examinations in a wide range of health-related topics including food hygiene and nutrition. It has set and examined standards of food hygiene skills since the 1960s. Most of the courses can be followed on a part-time basis and complement an additional programme of study.

Royal Society of Health

38A St. George's Drive, London SW1V 4BH; Tel: 020 7630 0121

The Royal Society sets standards and moderates examinations for a wide variety of nutrition and health issues. The courses are often used to complement a wider educational programme, although they can be taken individually. Courses include:

◆ Diploma in Nutrition;
◆ Certificate in Nutrition;
◆ Certificate in Essential Food Hygiene;
◆ Diploma in Food Hygiene Management;
◆ Certificate in Food Retailing.

Training and Enterprise Councils and Local Enterprise Companies (various locations)

Training and Enterprise Councils were a government initiative begun in 1990/91. There are 81 TECs in England and Wales, each dealing with a given territory. Their mission is to help local people and local business by maximizing human resource potential in business, enterprise and the local labour market. As a consequence, much of their work is in partnership with local key agencies, for example, colleges and employers. Local Enterprise Companies, of which there are 22, fulfil the same role in Scotland.

By investing in people and business, they are able to support Modern Apprenticeship schemes, promote good practice in business, assist businesses with training and development, act as an advisor and provide training. This unique service aids those unemployed and actively seeking employment, people with disabilities, school-leavers seeking retraining, and adults.

Wine and Spirit Education Trust Ltd

Five Kings House, 1 Queen Street Place, London EC4R 1QS; Tel: 020 7236 3551; www.wset.co.uk

An independent charity set up to educate all those employed in the wine and spirit trade, the Trust organizes courses, sets examinations and standards and liaises closely with catering organizations. It is not directly accredited with NCVQ because the NVQ system deals specifically with job competencies, the skills necessary to do a job. The Trust's qualifications are evidence of underpinning knowledge, the theory aspects about a range of products. As a guide, the Wine and Spirit Education Trust considers its three qualifications supply evidence of underpinning knowledge at the following NVQ levels:

◆ Certificate (= NVQ level 2);
◆ Higher Certificate (= NVQ level 3);
◆ Diploma (= NVQ level 4).

Other useful addresses

Academy of Culinary Arts, 517 Old York Road, London SW18 1TF; Tel: 020 8874 8500
Academy of Food and Wine Service, Burgoine House, 8 Lower Teddington Road, Kingston Upon Thames, Surrey KT1 4ER; Tel: 020 8943 1011

The Brewers and Licensed Retailers Association, 42 Portman Square, London WC1H 0BB; Tel: 020 7486 4831
British Dietetic Association, 7th Floor, Elizabeth House, 22 Suffolk Street, Queensway, Birmingham B1 1LS; Tel: 0121 616 4900
British Hospitality Association, Queens House, 55–60 Lincoln's Inn Fields, London WC2A 3BH; Tel: 020 7404 7744
British Institute of Innkeeping, Park House House, 24 Park Street, Camberley, Surrey GU15 3PL; Tel: 01276 684449
British Nutrition Foundation, High Holborn House, 52–54 High Holborn, London WC1V 6RQ; Tel: 020 7404 6504
British Tourist Authority, Thames Tower, Black's Road, Hammersmith, London W6 9EL; Tel: 020 8846 9000

Catering Managers Association of Great Britain and the Channel Islands, Mount Pleasant, Egton, Whitby, North Yorkshire YO21 1UE; Tel: 01947 895514
Cookery and Food Association, 1 Victoria Parade, 331 Sandycombe Road, Richmond, Surrey TW9 3NB; Tel: 020 8948 3870

Court of Master Sommeliers, 1 Seaway Close, Chelston, Torquay TQ2 6PY; Tel: 01803 605031
Craft Guild of Chefs, 1 Victoria Parade, 331 Sandycombe Road, Richmond, Surrey TW9 3NB; Tel: 020 8948 3870

European Catering Association, Bourne House, Horsell Park, Woking, Surrey GU21 4LY; Tel: 01483 765000

Federation of Bakers, 6 Catherine Street, London WC2B 5JW Tel: 020 7420 7190
Federation of Licensed Victuallers Association, 128 Bradford Road, Brighouse, West Yorkshire HD6 4AU; Tel: 01484 710534

The Guild of Food Writers, 48 Crabtree Lane, London SW6 6LW; Tel: 020 7610 1180

Institute of Food Science and Technology, 5 Cambridge Court, 210 Shepherd's Bush Road, London W6 7NL; Tel: 020 7603 6316
Institute of Masters of Wine, Five Kings House, 1 Queen St Place, London EC4R 1QS; Tel: 020 7236 4427
Institute of Travel and Tourism, 113 Victoria Street, St. Albans, Hertfordshire AL1 3TJ; Tel: 01727 854395
International Flight Catering Association, Surrey Place, Mill Lane, Godalming, Surrey GU7 1EY; Tel: 01483 419449
International Wine and Food Society, 9 Fitzmaurice Place, London WC1X 6JD; Tel: 020 7495 4191

National Association of Licensed House Managers, Transport House, Merchants Quay, Salford M5 2SG; Tel: 0161 848 3469

Restaurant Association, Africa House, 64–78 Kingsway, London WC2B 6AH; Tel: 020 7831 8727

Scottish Licensed Trade Association, 10 Walker Street, Edinburgh EH3 7LA; Tel: 0131 225 5169
Springboard, 1-3 Denmark Street, London WC2H 8LP; Tel: 020 7497 8654

The Tea Council Ltd, Sir John Lyon House, 5 High Timber Street, London EC4V 3NJ; Tel: 020 7248 1024

Tourism Society, 26 Chapter Street, London SW1P 4ND; Tel: 020 7834 0461

UK Bartenders Guild, Rosebank, Blackness, Scotland EH49 7NL; Tel: 01506 834448

Universities and Colleges Admissions Service (UCAS), PO Box 28, Cheltenham, Gloucestershire GL50 3SA; Tel: 01242 222444

The Vegan Society, Donald Watson House, 7 Battle Road, St Leonards-on-Sea, East Sussex TN37 7AA; Tel: 01424 427393

The Vegetarian Society, Parkdale, Dunham Road, Altrincham, Cheshire WA14 4QG; Tel: 0161 925 2000

Index

The Kogan Page *Careers in...* series

Careers in Accountancy *(6th edition)*
Careers in Architecture *(5th edition)*
Careers in Art and Design *(8th edition)*
Careers in Banking and Finance *(5th edition)*
Careers in Catering, Hotel Administration and Management
 (5th edition)
Careers in Computing and Information Technology
Careers in Environmental Conservation *(6th edition)*
Careers in Film and Video *(5th edition)*
Careers in Hairdressing and Beauty Therapy *(7th edition)*
Careers in Journalism *(8th edition)*
Careers in the Law *(8th edition)*
Careers in Marketing, Advertising and Public Relations
 (6th edition)
Careers in Medicine, Dentistry and Mental Health *(7th edition)*
Careers in Music
Careers in Nursing and Related Professions *(8th edition)*
Careers in the Police Service *(5th edition)*
Careers in Publishing and Bookselling *(2nd edition)*
Careers in Retailing *(6th edition)*
Careers in Secretarial and Office Work *(7th edition)*
Careers in Social Care *(7th edition)*
Careers in Sport *(7th edition)*
Careers in Teaching *(7th edition)*
Careers in Television and Radio *(7th edition)*
Careers in the Theatre *(6th edition)*
Careers in the Travel Industry *(6th edition)*
Careers Using English
Careers Using Languages *(8th edition)*
Careers Working with Animals *(8th edition)*
Careers in Working with Children and Young People
 (7th edition)
Careers Working Outdoors *(7th edition)*